Every Day Is

Saturday

ALSO BY JERRY ZEZIMA

"Leave It to Boomer: A Look at Life, Love and Parenthood
by the Very Model of the Modern Middle-Age Man"

"The Empty Nest Chronicles: How to Have Fun (and Stop
Annoying Your Spouse) After the Kids Move Out"

"Grandfather Knows Best: A Geezer's Guide to Life, Immaturity,
and Learning How to Change Diapers All Over Again"

"Nini and Poppie's Excellent Adventures: Grandkids,
Wine Clubs, and Other Ways to Keep Having Fun"

Every Day Is Saturday

Sleeping Late, Playing With
the Grandchildren, Surviving the Quarantine,
and Other Joys of Retirement

JERRY ZEZIMA

EVERY DAY IS SATURDAY
SLEEPING LATE, PLAYING WITH THE
GRANDCHILDREN, SURVIVING THE QUARANTINE,
AND OTHER JOYS OF RETIREMENT

iUniverse books may be ordered through booksellers or by contacting:

iUniverse
1663 Liberty Drive
Bloomington, IN 47403
www.iuniverse.com
844-349-9409

Because of the dynamic nature of the Internet, any web addresses or links contained in this book may have changed since publication and may no longer be valid. The views expressed in this work are solely those of the author and do not necessarily reflect the views of the publisher, and the publisher hereby disclaims any responsibility for them.

Any people depicted in stock imagery provided by Getty Images are models, and such images are being used for illustrative purposes only. Certain stock imagery © Getty Images.

Back cover photograph copyright 2020 by Lauren Robert-Demolaize www.laurendemolaizephotography.com

ISBN: 978-1-6632-0563-6 (sc)
ISBN: 978-1-6632-0564-3 (e)

Print information available on the last page.

iUniverse rev. date: 08/03/2020

PRAISE FOR JERRY ZEZIMA

"Jerry Zezima's columns are terrific."

— Max Pross, Emmy Award-winning writer
for "The Simpsons" and "Seinfeld"

"Who could envision Jerry Zezima emerging as the Will Rogers of retirement? Only anyone who's ever read his laugh-out-loud columns on the absurdities of daily life. Inside these pages, he riffs on everything from the perils of lugging furniture as a geezer to the quiet hell of a visit to the local Social Security office and the joy of an outing — with his wife, no less! — to the dump, the old guy's Disney World if ever there was one."

— Kevin Cowherd, former Baltimore Sun humor columnist and
sportswriter and the author of "When the Crowd Didn't Roar" and
the New York Times bestselling novel for young readers "Hothead"

"Jerry Zezima notices the funny parts of life. For that we, his delighted readers, are grateful. Celebrating the moments of surprise, recognition, and community, Jerry is the right writer when we need to remember that every day has something glorious to offer, if only we know where to look."

— Gina Barreca, University of Connecticut professor and author
of "They Used to Call Me Snow White, But I Drifted"

"Jerry Zezima is an observer of life's simplicities. He has the wonderful ability to put a humorous spin on the things we do every day. A trip to the dump, getting a haircut, baking a cake ... who knew there were funny and heartwarming moments to be found in all of these?"

— Lonnie Quinn, chief weather anchor,
WCBS-TV, and Emmy Award winner

"Jerry Zezima is funny through and through. Even when he's not trying, the jokes and wordplay keep coming. He just can't help himself. I hope he gets professional help."

"In his endearing and funny new book, 'Every Day Is Saturday,' Jerry Zezima makes us laugh once again — this time as he recounts his retirement shenanigans as husband, father, and grandfather. This is just the kind of positive story we need about life, laughter, and the love of family. Bravo!"

"We don't know how Jerry manages to find the funny side of everything … but he does. Our readers laugh. So do we."

"Jerry Zezima has retired from his day job, but he hasn't retired from being hilarious. So we who love his always-SOCIAL humor have the SECURITY of knowing we can continue to enjoy his writing. You'll love this funny and heartwarming book."

"Jerry Zezima is the dad — and grandpa — we all wish we had. With warmth and grace, he has a knack for elevating the everyday and, in an age when it is *de rigueur* to mock others, he laughs only at himself. In 'Every Day Is Saturday: Sleeping Late, Playing With the Grandchildren, Surviving the Quarantine, and Other Joys of Retirement,' he proves once again that he's the Father of Funny, the Grandpa of Guffaws, and the unrepentant Crown Prince of the Pun. Join Jerry as he lives, loves, and lurches toward decrepitude, laughing all the way."

— Dawn Weber, national award-winning humor columnist and author of "I Love You. Now Go Away: Confessions of a Woman With a Smartphone"

CONTENTS

DEDICATION

To my wife, Sue, and our grandchildren, Chloe, Lilly, Xavier, Zoe, and Quinn, who make retirement fun.

And to my hometown paper, the Stamford Advocate, which gave me a chance, a column, and a career.

ACKNOWLEDGMENTS

To my daughters, Katie and Lauren, and their husbands, Dave and Guillaume, thanks for giving me a purpose in life, which is to be The Manny, a master babysitter and a devoted grandfather whose shockingly immature shenanigans with your children have indoctrinated them into the Cult of Poppie.

To Lee Steele, features editor at Hearst Connecticut Media Group, thanks for being such a great guy and for running my column in the Sunday magazine, even though there is no question that it is contributing to the decline of the newspaper industry.

To Zach Finken and all the other good folks at Tribune News Service, thanks for distributing my column to papers nationwide and abroad. You are just adding to the aforementioned problem, but I appreciate it.

To Marty Cain, Christine Colborne, and the rest of the team at iUniverse, thanks for publishing this book, my fifth for the house. You have yet to wise up, and I am grateful.

To the many others both in and out of journalism who helped and encouraged me during my career, I can only say that countless people would blame you for the sad fact that I am still inflicting myself on the reading public, but I thank you. Now get back to work because — ha! ha! — I don't have to.

INTRODUCTION

On the first day of the rest of my life, I rolled over and went back to sleep.

For forty-three years, four months, and seventeen days, but who's counting, I had set the alarm for an ungodly hour, which was so early that even God wasn't up. Then I would stagger into the office, mumble "good morning" to no one in particular, because no one in particular would listen to me, plop my posterior into a worn-out chair, and roll over and go back to sleep at my desk.

Now that I am retired, I don't have to get out of bed to do the same thing.

One of the best things about being retired is that you don't have to wear pants every day. If you try that at work, you will end up being unemployed, but without a buyout. What you will receive is a get-out: No severance, just leave. And don't let the door hit you in the boxer shorts on the way out.

The buyout, which came with a generous package that did not, unfortunately, include beer, was a surprise to me and my colleagues, many of whom are fellow baby boomers who had been go-getters in their day (mine was March 30, 1976, when I began my career) but who had grown weary of the daily grind.

As an army of anxious employees crammed into the auditorium, the stunning announcement was made: The company was offering buyouts.

Naturally, there were questions:

How much would we get? Could we apply for unemployment? What would happen with our 401(k)s?

I raised my hand.

"If someone is injured sprinting to the human resources department to apply for a buyout," I asked, "would it be covered under our medical plan?"

Everybody laughed. Nobody answered.

When the meeting was over, I texted my wife, Sue, with one word: "BUYOUT!"

Eight seconds later, she replied: "How much?"

It was enough for me to sprint to the human resources department to apply.

Three weeks later, I was without a job.

It raised an important question: How could I stop working when I never really started? Also, what would I do with myself? What would Sue do with me? Would I become so fantastically annoying that I'd have to work part time as a stock boy in a grocery store just to get out of the house?

The answers were easy: My job may have ended, but my career hasn't. For twenty-two years, I was an editor at Newsday. For all of that time and for the previous twenty-one years, I was a writer for my hometown paper, the Stamford Advocate, including more than three decades as a columnist whose work, I am proud to say, has no redeeming social value.

I quit the editing and staggering into the office but not the rest.

From home, I have continued to write my nationally syndicated humor column for Hearst Connecticut Media Group and Tribune News Service of Chicago. I have written this book, my fifth. Like the first four, it's a crime against literature. And I am writing a sitcom based on my work. If you think TV is bad now, wait until my show gets on the air.

I had long said that I could do a lot of work if I didn't have to go to work. Now I don't. And I am working harder — and more happily — than ever.

But my most important job involves my grandchildren, Chloe, Lilly, Xavier, Zoe, and Quinn. They range in age from seven to one. And they're all more mature than I am.

You have to wonder who babysits whom.

Chloe and Lilly, the daughters of our younger daughter, Lauren, and her husband, Guillaume, live about forty-five minutes from our house on Long Island, New York.

Xavier, Zoe, and Quinn are the children of our older daughter, Katie, and her husband, Dave. They also live about forty-five minutes away (by plane) in Washington, D.C.

Grandkids are a big part of retirement. So are spouses. Sue and I have been married for forty-two years. If it weren't for her, I would be either dead or in prison. She's the backbone of the family, my soulmate, a woman who, for putting up with me for so long, deserves to be the first living person canonized by the Catholic Church. I deserve to be shot from a cannon.

Sue has been a teacher's assistant for three decades. Working with children is the highest calling. It's the world's most important job — except, of course, for being my doctor.

Sue keeps busy by keeping me busy.

"I am making a to-do list for you," she often says.

I don't make a big to-do out of it. I just do it. Marriage, after all, is dear season: "Yes, dear."

That goes especially for retirement.

But life is good, as it has always been. It's different now, but even better.

You will read a lot more about it in the rest of this book, which contains absolutely true stories about real people, not just family members but friends, former co-workers, and even complete strangers.

Of course, all of these retirement chores can really tire a guy out. So please excuse me while I roll over and go back to sleep.

CHAPTER 1

(How did I ever get into journalism? And how did I manage to stay in it for more than four decades without destroying the entire industry? Here's the story.)

"My Semi-brilliant Career"

I knew I wanted to be a writer when I was in high school. My decision could be encapsulated in one word:

Algebra.

Here, as I dimly recall, which is how I recall most things these days, is the typical algebra problem:

> *The Smiths are leaving New York for Boston at nine a.m., averaging fifty-five miles per hour. The Joneses are leaving Boston for New York at ten a.m., averaging fifty miles per hour.*
>
> *Question: At what point in the two-hundred-mile journey will they pass each other?*

You can try to figure it out, but I'll save you the time. Here is the correct answer:

WHO THE HELL CARES?!

Anyone who cranes his neck to see when his friends will pass him on the other side of the road, instead of keeping his eyes on his own side, is a menace to society and ought to have his driver's license revoked.

I was never very good in subjects where you actually had to know the answers. I was much better in subjects where you could bluff your way through.

Like English composition.

In one class at my high school, Stamford Catholic in my hometown of Stamford, Connecticut, we had to write an essay on a particular subject, then get up in the front of the room to read it.

Nobody wanted to do this. Except me.

Everybody took it seriously. Except me.

I wrote the silliest, stupidest, craziest, funniest stuff I could think of. When I got up in front of the class to read my essay, I got big laughs.

A light bulb went off in my otherwise empty head: I could do this for a living.

My teachers at Catholic High were very supportive. They were too kind to say so explicitly, but they strongly implied that I was spectacularly unqualified to do anything else.

I was the class clown. My professional goal was to be silly and irresponsible and actually get paid for it.

How could I accomplish this? I had read the great humor columnists Art Buchwald and Erma Bombeck in my hometown paper, the Stamford Advocate.

I resolved to write a humor column, too. It would be like doing stand-up comedy, except I wouldn't have to show up.

Also attending Stamford Catholic High School, Class of 1971, was a cute girl named Sue Pikero. I saw her one day in the cafeteria and instantly made a personal goal: I would marry her. She didn't know this at the time. In fact, she was dating a guy who was one of my best friends. Needless to say, but I'll say it anyway, he is no longer one of my best friends.

When I found out Sue would be going to Saint Michael's College in Colchester, Vermont, I applied, too. To my eternal gratitude, the school lowered its otherwise high standards and accepted me. I graduated, along with Sue, in the Class of 1975.

A year later, I walked into the office of the Stamford Advocate and I announced that I wanted a job.

The editor, Roland Blais, asked what experience I had. I told him I didn't have any. I didn't write for the high school paper and I didn't write for the college paper.

So Mr. Blais gave me a test. Fortunately, it wasn't algebra. It was general knowledge — grammar, history, current events — and I did well enough because I was hired. But there were some questions to which I did not know the answers. Instead of leaving them blank or taking half-hearted guesses, I remembered what I did on that essay in high school:

I wrote the silliest, stupidest, craziest, funniest stuff I could think of. Later, Mr. Blais said that's what got me the job.

"It showed signs of creativity," he added.

I was about to say that I didn't think you were supposed to make stuff up in a newspaper, but for once in my life, I kept my mouth shut.

Frankly, I had no business being in the newspaper business. I couldn't get a job today with my lack of experience. But just as I did in high school, I bluffed my way through. I've been doing it my whole life. I hope this is a good lesson to all you young people out there.

I started as a copyboy. My job consisted mainly of getting coffee for the editors. Three months later, perhaps dissatisfied with the quality of the java from the greasy spoon down the street, Mr. Blais promoted me to city-side reporter. I covered the police beat, which entailed going to the cop shop and getting the daily blotter (I was always amazed that I wasn't in it). I also wrote news features, including my first bylined piece, a front-page story about the closing of a deli frequented by the publisher, a crusty old coot who, I was told, had a great interest in my piece.

I was immensely relieved when he told me that he liked it. This meant I would stay on the payroll. The money wasn't bountiful but came in handy because, after dating briefly, Sue and I were engaged. In 1978, I achieved the personal goal I had set in high school: I married her.

Around the time of our engagement, there was an opening on the sports staff. I applied and got the job. For the next eight years, I was a sportswriter, covering everything from Little League baseball to professional football.

In 1984, I got out of sports and became an assistant metro editor. Nine months later, the bosses, who now included managing editor Barry

Hoffman and executive features editor Joyce Gabriel, wanted me to go to features.

Here was my chance to achieve my professional goal, also made in high school, of being a humor columnist. For the only time in my life, I made a demand: I would move to features if I got a column. Barry and Joyce, bless their hearts, gave me one.

My first column ran in May of 1985. The following year, I won first place for humor in the National Society of Newspaper Columnists' writing contest. I have since won six more humor awards from the NSNC, of which I was president from 2014 to 2016.

When I began my column, Sue was home with Katie, who was born in 1980, and Lauren, who was born in 1982. When the girls started school, so did Sue. She got a job as a teacher's assistant in the Stamford public school system.

Sue and the girls became the primary focus of my column. For years I have written about family foibles and the funny little things of everyday life. It's been a gold mine of material.

One of the nicest compliments I ever got was from a woman who said, "I think your columns are very funny. But what I really like about them is that you never put down your wife or use your kids for cheap laughs."

I am not above trying to get cheap laughs, but they are at my expense.

Readers have also told me that it's like I am living in their house.

"Actually," I reply, "I *am* living in your house. And you're out of beer. Please go buy some more."

From the beginning, my column has run in newspapers across the country and around the world, first through the Los Angeles Times-Washington Post News Service and then through Tribune News Service, with which I am still happily affiliated.

If you have ever wondered why the newspaper business is in trouble, it would be because of me.

In 1997, I was faced with a major decision. Katie and Lauren were approaching college, the cost of which rivaled the gross national product of Finland. I needed to make more money. I loved working at the

Stamford Advocate, but it's a relatively small paper and I was at the top of the pay scale as a writer.

So I applied to Newsday, the daily paper on Long Island, New York, as a copy editor. Newsday was owned by the Times Mirror Company, which also owned the Stamford Advocate, so there was a connection.

A more direct connection was Jack Millrod, a terrific guy whom I knew when he was senior news editor on the copy desk at the Stamford Advocate and who was now an executive news editor at Newsday. He arranged for me to have a weeklong tryout.

On the last day, I edited a local story that included the publisher of Newsday. I noticed a typo in his name, fixed it, and brought it to the attention of Jack and some of the other managers, who were so grateful that I didn't allow such a monumental gaffe to get in the paper that they hired me. Bob Keane, assistant managing editor for administration and a terrific guy, too, made my employment official when he got a kick out of an answer I put down on the application. Where it said, "Salary," I wrote, "Yes."

"Recruiting and hiring you was one of the better moves I made," Bob, a longtime retiree, said in an email when I was writing this book.

For the next twenty-two years, I worked on the copy desk with people who were as wonderful as my colleagues at the Stamford Advocate. That included Jack, who was a great first boss. Unfortunately, except for a four-month stretch in 1997, when I filled in for a writer who was on sabbatical, and a later brief stretch online, Newsday didn't run my column. It's a very good paper, just like the Stamford Advocate, but if you're a humorist, Newsday is the last place on earth you want to be. Still, I enjoyed my time there.

Sue, meanwhile, got a job as a teacher's assistant at a private preschool on Long Island. The irony is that she was vice president of the teacher's assistants' union in Stamford and helped negotiate a pension for the members. It took effect the year after she left.

I commuted from Stamford to the Newsday office in Melville, New York, and back again every weekday for fifteen months before Sue and I bought a house on Long Island. I actually kissed the ground the day we moved in.

Katie and Lauren went through college and moved out of the house, making Sue and me empty nesters. Then they got married. Then they had children, which meant Sue and I were grandparents. There's nothing like it.

The grandkids also became fodder for my column, which I have continued to write on a freelance basis. Eventually, the column moved to the Sunday magazine of Hearst Connecticut Media Group, which owns the Advocate and several other papers in the state, meaning the column gets even wider exposure.

In 2010, I wrote my first book, "Leave It to Boomer." I followed in 2013 with "The Empty Nest Chronicles," in 2016 with "Grandfather Knows Best," and in 2018 with "Nini and Poppie's Excellent Adventures."

Since I hadn't killed the publishing industry, I wrote this book. Thanks for buying it. I hope you know that it's too late to get a refund.

I was still in my day job as an editor, certain that I'd be working posthumously, when Newsday offered that buyout. I was sixty-five. The package would carry me past the Social Security peak of sixty-six, so I took it.

Now here I am, a happy retiree, a good career behind me, the best part of it continuing, and the rest of my life ahead of me.

Not bad for the class clown in high school.

CHAPTER 2

(When I retired, I was a free man, wondering how I was going to fill my free time. Answer: Grandchildren! They make retirement grand.)

"The Grandkid Olympics"

As a lean, mean geezer machine, I have managed to keep my boyish figure all these years by strictly adhering to Zezima's First Rule of Physical Fitness: Exercise and health food will kill you.

That's why my regimen is limited to twelve-ounce curls, which are performed with bottles containing corn, hops, barley, water, and other healthful ingredients; the avoidance of all vegetables except, of course, myself; and a daily glass of red wine, which is, according to my doctor, over-the-counter heart medicine.

But I have reached the age (old enough to know better) where I really should be more active than getting up twice a night to go to the bathroom.

That's where my grandchildren come in.

Chloe, Lilly, and Xavier are the proprietors of Poppie's Gym, a floating health club and potential emergency care facility that is situated wherever the kids and I happen to be.

The various sites include my house, their houses, the backyards of the aforementioned places, the kiddie pool, the playground, the vineyard, the apple orchard, the amusement park, and whatever store, outlet, or mall where my wife and/or daughters are shopping while I am watching or, more likely, chasing the children.

Activities include walking, running, hopping, skipping, jumping, crawling, scampering, splashing, dancing, throwing, batting, kicking, and weightlifting. If there were a grandfather competition in the Olympics, I would have won gold in all these events and appeared on boxes of Wheaties, my smiling visage covered with an oxygen mask.

I ramped up the exertion level when all three grandchildren visited. It was invigorating, especially when I hoisted Chloe, who weighs almost fifty pounds; Xavier, who tips the scales at thirty pounds; and Lilly, the peanut of the bunch at twenty-three pounds but whose squirminess in my arms amounts to a clean and jerk, the former involving a diaper change and the latter describing me.

Then there was the hundred-inch dash, in which I chased Chloe and Lilly across the family room and back again so many times that a calculator would have exploded like the Hindenburg.

Xavier preferred the biathlon, which entailed playing peekaboo and then running around the room with Poppie on his heels. It's a miracle I didn't wear out my heels.

On numerous occasions, all the kids wanted to take my hand and play with me individually. This would require me either to be three people (as Sue would say, isn't one enough?) or to have three hands, which in the winter would leave me one glove short.

After several days, the Olympics were over and Xavier went back home. Sue and I will soon get on a plane to visit him and the athletics will continue. We often see Chloe and Lilly, who live only about forty-five minutes away, so Poppie will be sure to keep in tip-top shape.

In fact, shortly after the sporting events had ceased, I went to the doctor for a checkup. My heart rate and blood pressure were perfect, my weight was normal, and overall I was declared a remarkable physical specimen.

"What do you do to stay so fit?" the doctor asked.

"I play with my grandchildren," I replied.

"Keep it up," he advised. "It beats getting up twice a night to go to the bathroom."

"Mr. Poppie Goes to Washington"

After returning from Washington, D.C., where I spent a lot of time coloring with crayons, playing with blocks, and going down slides, making me more productive than anyone else there, I can say with great pride and total accuracy that Xavier is the smartest and most mature person in the nation's capital.

And it turned out that I was the most influential. That's because my lobbying efforts to have fun paid dividends not only with Xavier, but with his friends Hayden and Walter.

My influence even extended to grown-ups such as the woman who carded me when I bought wine in a grocery store and the bartender who didn't card me when I ordered a beer but did say that Washington is undergoing a booze renaissance.

I was happy to contribute to this encouraging development during the five days when Sue and I visited Xavier, Katie, and Dave.

And I built up quite a thirst playing with Xavier, who has an impressive collection of coloring books and approximately a thousand crayons, as well as a boxful of blocks that we used to build planes, trains, and automobiles. It gave me hope that he will grow up to be either a great artist or secretary of transportation.

But I really exerted myself at the playground, where Xavier met up with his buddy Hayden, who took an instant liking to me, probably because he sensed that I was on his intellectual level, and wanted me to take him down each of the park's several slides several times each.

This presented a daunting challenge to a geezer whose pathetic struggle to climb stairs, crawl through child-size tunnels, and whoosh down twisting plastic surfaces with a squirming toddler on his lap nearly resulted in an ambulance ride to the emergency room.

Naturally, Xavier wanted me to do the same with him.

"Follow me," I said to the two boys. "I'm the Pied Poppie."

Later, it was my turn to follow our little family band when we went to a grocery store to buy ingredients for dinner (Dave is a marvelous cook) and purchase some wine: a bottle of red and a bottle of white, with no apologies to Billy Joel.

"May I please see your ID?" asked a very nice cashier named Laura, who appeared to be about forty years younger than I am.

"Really?!" I squealed. "You're actually carding me? Do I look that young?"

Laura smiled and said, "I have to do this to everyone."

"Do you want to see my AARP card?" I asked disappointedly.

"Your driver's license will do," said Laura.

From there, we went to a market that had a bakery, a bar, and a community library.

I bellied up to the libation portion of the establishment and ordered a beer from Vince, who said he also works at a distillery that makes whiskey, gin, and vodka.

"Washington is having a booze renaissance," he told me.

"That explains things," I replied.

Before I could finish my beer, Xavier and his BFF, Walter, who was there with his parents, wanted me to sit down with them and read the children's book "What Do People Do All Day?" by Richard Scarry.

"Poppie doesn't do a heck of a lot," I said before launching into the delightful text, which the boys loved.

All in all, I had a wonderful time in the nation's capital, and my faith was restored in a city where a trio of little boys showed that people could actually get along with each other.

It's what I would call a kid renaissance.

"Come and Meet Those Dancing Feet"

When it comes to dancing, I have two left feet, which makes it extremely difficult to buy shoes. If I were on "Dancing With the Stars," the judges would all give me perfect scores — of zero. Len Goodman would add insult to injury by saying that only an injury could improve my dancing.

But take it from me, Dread Astaire: I know a winning performance when I see one. And I just happened to see one when I attended a dance recital starring Chloe and Lilly.

They weren't technically the stars because they were among a cast of dozens in a show whose theme was "The Wizard of Oz." But they did stand out because they executed their routines perfectly.

Their grandfather, after his routine, would have been executed.

When I was a kid, I took dancing lessons at the Phil Jones School of Dance in Stamford, but I was so bad that: (a) none of the girls wanted to be my partner and (b) the school closed.

Sue and I took dancing lessons before Katie and Dave's wedding, but like cramming for a geometry test, I forgot everything as soon as the lessons were over. At the wedding, Sue and I did basic geometry by dancing in circles.

We didn't even bother with dancing lessons before Lauren and Guillaume's wedding.

At the recital, which drew a large crowd, the girls wore colorful tutus. I didn't wear a tutu, which would have been tutu much for my family to bear. Besides, my outfit would have been ruined in the rain because I had to drop off Sue at the door and leave the car about half a mile away.

"I guess they don't have ballet parking," I said when we took our seats.

Everyone ignored me. And for good reason: The show was about to begin!

Shortly after the curtain went up, the little kids, including Lilly, pranced out and formed a line. Lilly, dressed in blue with a bright red bow in her hair, was last but not least. She wiggled and sashayed, earning appreciative chuckles from the audience.

To the strains of "Ding Dong! The Witch Is Dead," the group exited stage left. Lilly clapped for herself. The crowd clapped back.

Not long afterward, another group, including Chloe, came out. Each girl was carrying a giant peppermint lollipop. Chloe's was as tall as she is. In her black and red outfit, she danced to the beat of — you guessed it — "Lollipop."

"Lollipop, lollipop, oh, lolli, lolli, lolli, lollipop!" went the piped-in lyrics, over and over, filling my normally empty head.

Chloe and the other girls put their right feet out, then their left, bent over, and jumped. It was all perfectly timed.

Applause filled the auditorium. It did so again as the troupe exited to "We're Off the See the Wizard." Chloe waved to the crowd. Everybody waved in return.

"That was great!" I gushed when the ninety-minute show was over. "And Chloe and Lilly were fantastic."

Befitting their new status as theater celebrities, the girls got flowers backstage and posed for pictures. The only thing they didn't do was sign autographs, probably because nobody thought to bring crayons.

I can see them in a Broadway musical or the Joffrey Ballet. They might even be on "Dancing With the Stars."

Or they could open their own school of dance. Their grandfather will be the first one to take lessons.

"Field Day Comes Off My Bucket List"

Anyone who knows me and is willing to admit it, which severely narrows the field, knows that I always have a field day with my grandchildren. But I had a real one at Chloe's elementary school, where I was a volunteer for — what are the odds? — Field Day.

I signed up for the water relay, one of several events that would give me a heart attack if I competed in them. But it was the only one that proved, as if anyone needed verification, that I am all wet.

Chloe and her kindergarten classmates were the youngest of the participants, all of whom showed an unbeatable combination of athletic ability and sportsmanship.

I will modestly admit that I was a pretty fair athlete in my day. Unfortunately, that day was June 12, 1960, when I was Chloe's age. I have been regressing ever since.

My partner in officiating the water relay was Jimmy Smith, with whom I worked for many years (that's only half right: he worked, I didn't) and whose daughter, Sarah, a second-grader, also was one of the participants.

The object of the relay was for students to dip a plastic cup into a bucket of water, run to another bucket several yards away, dump the cup of water into the second bucket, and run back to the first bucket, where it was the next student's turn. This was repeated until either time or water ran out and I was splashed so much that I looked like I had just emerged from a deep-sea expedition.

"I'm glad we put this on our bucket list," I told Jimmy. "I just hope we don't kick the bucket."

"Then people could say we were in the bucket brigade," he replied helpfully.

Jimmy used the watch on his phone (only Dick Tracy has a phone on his watch) to time each relay, which lasted for five minutes.

Two teams — blue and yellow — competed in the various events, which included obstacle course, potato sack race, hippity-hop race, hoop relay, and fifty-yard sprint.

Unwittingly, which is how I do almost everything, I wore a blue T-shirt. It was perfect because blue is Chloe's favorite color (along with pink) and she was on the blue team.

But she wasn't in the first few relays. Instead, she was competing in other events, being cheered on by Lauren and Lilly.

My job was to stand by the blue team's second bucket and exhort the players by saying: "Hurry up!" (if they weren't hurrying), "That's OK!" (if they slipped or got more water on my shoes than in the bucket), and "Good job!" (if they did a good job, which all of them did).

One of the best players was Sarah, a sweet and funny girl who is a natural athlete.

Either because of or in spite of my dubious coaching efforts, the blue team won most of the relays.

During one of the breaks, I went back to my car to get a wide-brimmed hat to shield me from the relentless sun.

"Are you going on safari?" Jimmy asked.

"Safari, so good!" I retorted.

"With us," he suggested, "all that's missing is the third Stooge."

Until the last relay, Chloe had been missing, too. But she showed up with her blue team classmates for the final run. I asked her to help demonstrate what to do and she pulled it off flawlessly.

During the relay, all the kids did a great job. That was especially true of Chloe, who ran fast and didn't spill a drop.

It was a fitting conclusion to a Field Day of Dreams.

"Pooling Our Resources"

Now that we are in the dog days of summer, and the heat makes dogs pant so much that they don't even wear pants, it can safely be said that most people would give their right arms for a pool, which kind of defeats the purpose because they'd end up swimming in circles.

Nonetheless, a pool not only provides watery fun for homeowners — as well as their neighbors, who may or may not have been invited for a swim and often refuse to leave, causing the owners to either call the cops or put the house on the market — but it is a sure sign of status.

This leads neighbors without such luxuries to ask the following questions:

How can the Zezimas afford a pool?

Why don't they invite us for a swim?

And, most pertinent, what the hell is gunite?

According to Merriam-Webster, who has a dictionary-shaped pool, gunite is "a building material consisting of a mixture of cement, sand, and water that is sprayed onto a mold" and is used in luxury swimming pools.

I don't want to brag, because the neighbors might hear me, but we have not one, not two, but three pools.

That they are of the kiddie variety is beside the point.

The kiddies are Chloe and Lilly, who love to frolic in four inches of grass-flecked water while Sue and I sit poolside in rickety beach chairs, attired stylishly in saggy T-shirts and ketchup-stained shorts while quaffing lukewarm summer ales straight out of the bottle, a sure sign of status.

Instead of gunite, these pools are made of good, old-fashioned, earth-destroying plastic and come in small, medium, and large.

The biggest is seventy inches across and is lined with pictures of dinosaurs, which probably reminds the kids of their grandparents. It is filled not with special water from massive delivery trucks used by the rich and famous for their elaborate pools, but with what comes out of a garden hose. It is invariably cold enough to give a walrus pneumonia.

We use an energy-efficient heating system powered by either the sun or, if it is playing peekaboo with the clouds, boiled water from a teakettle.

Whereas the elite surround their pools with sophisticated landscaping that includes colorful pavers, sculpted rocks, and finely manicured hillocks, we have a natural look featuring a broken walkway that hasn't been repaired in more than a dozen years.

On one side is monstrous vegetation that includes an out-of-control holly bush, two ugly hydrangeas, and Sue's garden, which has so far produced only a handful of hot peppers and even fewer tomatoes. On the other side is an above-ground oil tank that is utterly useless for heating pool water.

You may have seen how Hollywood stars adorn their pools with elaborate waterfalls or artificial geysers that shoot water high enough to splash their private jets.

We have a little round sprinkler with plastic flowers. It sends water about ten feet into the air. The girls like to run under the falling spray, which sometimes gets cut off if there is a kink in the hose. It is my job to fix the problem and get soaked in the process.

This vastly amuses my granddaughters, who then want me to stand in ankle-deep pool water with them and play with their toys. These aren't battleship-size floats but squirt guns and action figures we otherwise keep in a soggy shopping bag.

For the girls' next pool party, Sue has gone all out and bought a box of ice pops. The neighbors, I am sure, will be jealous.

"Something's Fishy in Our House"

Over the years, the fish population of our humble home has rivaled that of the Seven Seas, which is no fluke considering that the average lifespan of our fine finny friends has been approximately the length of the Super Bowl halftime show.

When Katie and Lauren were kids, our goldfish would go belly-up so often that you could set your watch by them, although only if your watch was waterproof.

As two little girls sobbed uncontrollably, Sue and I would perform a solemn toilet-side service that involved flushing the deceased to kingdom come.

We did have one fish, however, that lived a good, long life. His name was Curly. He was the bowl mate of Moe and Larry, who died within minutes of each other, probably in a suicide pact. Curly lived for weeks, only to meet a tragic demise.

One day I opened a kitchen cabinet and a bottle of vitamins fell out. It plummeted into the fish bowl and brained Curly.

"You killed our fish!" Katie and Lauren wailed.

Naturally, I felt terrible and offered them comforting words: "They were Mommy's vitamins."

We had no more fish until recently, when Chloe said she wanted us to get a fish for our house. Lilly eagerly concurred.

Their fish, Igor, lives at their house.

"You have to get one, too," Chloe said.

So we went to a nearby pet store on a fishing expedition.

"I want a girl fish," Chloe said. "She has to be pink. And I want to name her Camilla."

"Like Camilla Parker Bowles?" Sue asked, referring to Prince Charles's wife.

"No," said Chloe, who doesn't pay attention to the royal family. "She'll be Camilla Parker Zezima."

"And," I chimed in, "she'll live in the Camilla Parker bowl."

Chloe picked a light pink betta fish with dark pink fins. We got matching pink pebbles for the bottom of the bowl. We also got some fish food.

At the checkout counter, a cashier named Rufus inquired about the size of our fish bowl, which held sixteen ounces of water.

"You should get a tank that holds at least two and a half gallons," Rufus said. "Think of the fish's quality of life."

Unfortunately, Camilla's life wasn't long. She lasted forty-eight hours.

Chloe and Lilly, who had gone back to their house, where Igor, a blue boy betta, still swims happily in a sixteen-ounce bowl, were blissfully unaware that Camilla now resided in the suburban equivalent of Davy Jones's Locker.

I went back to the pet store and bought another betta that looks exactly like Camilla except that it's a male.

"I guess you could say the fish is gender-fluid," I told a salesman named Matt.

He agreed, noting that Chloe and Lilly would never know the difference. Then he sold me a one-gallon bowl.

"I'm going to put it on the liquor cabinet," I said, "so I can say he drinks like a fish."

At the checkout counter, a cashier named Mary told me that she had a betta male that lived for twelve years.

"His name was Skipper," Mary said. "He was exactly the color of your fish. And he was really sweet. He would come up to the surface so I could pet him. Sadly, he passed on. They don't live forever."

So far, the new Camilla has lived about a month. And, sure enough, Chloe and Lilly were none the wiser when they came over for a visit.

"I want to bring Igor to your house so he can have a sleepover with Camilla," Chloe said.

"I don't know about that," I whispered to Sue. "I'm afraid they'll end up sleeping with the fishes."

"New Grandkids Double the Fun"

There was a time when I was a two-fisted drinker, with a bottle in each hand and one large mouth to fill.

Now I am a two-fisted feeder, with a bottle in each hand and two small mouths to fill. That's what happened when Sue and I met our new twin grandchildren, Zoe and Quinn. Katie had given birth to the dynamic duo three weeks before Sue and I visited for seven days and (more important) nights, during which we helped Katie and Dave with babysitting Zoe, Quinn, and their big brother, Xavier, a sweet boy who loves his little siblings even more than he loves playing with me, which he did constantly at home, at a friend's house, and at a birthday party to which I, a bigger kid than any of the toddler guests, was invited.

The two bottles came into play when I fed Zoe and her younger (by twenty-five minutes) brother, Quinn, both of whom have healthy appetites that must be sated simultaneously to keep them on the same schedule.

This entailed, often between the wee small hours of one and four a.m., placing them on either side of me while using an ingenious invention called My Brest Friend, a nursing pillow that wraps around the feeder to ensure that always the twins shall eat.

I did double duty several times and even did quadruple duty (two twin feedings in one night) twice. I also did double doody (dual diaper detail) each time I did double duty, always before the feedings but sometimes directly afterward, too, which is doubly daunting for a geezer working on precious little sleep.

The greatest challenge was getting the bottles into both mouths and keeping the babies balanced while each guzzled between two and four ounces of one-hundred percent, all-natural mother's milk.

At halftime, there was burping. The babies also had to be burped, then fed the remainder of their meal, after which further eructations had to be coaxed before they could be swaddled (the only part at which I did not excel) and put back in their bassinets to sleep it off while I attempted to do the same on a nearby couch.

Two hours later, it was feeding time again.

Katie, who is nursing, had the most important role, of course. Dave did double duty with the pillow, but Sue never got the hang of it because, she said, "I'm too short." During the day, she fed either Zoe or Quinn while I fed the other.

Xavier provided moral support, saying hello to his infant siblings and kissing them in a touching display of brotherly love.

He also provided moral support to Sue and me. Xavier helped Sue make blueberry bread and meatball pizza, which he scarfed down for breakfast and dinner, respectively. And he helped me be uncharacteristically useful by reading to him, driving his toy trucks and trains, and engaging in spirited games of hide-and-seek.

"Xavier has joined the Cult of Poppie," Katie remarked, noting that Chloe and Lilly are already members and that Zoe and Quinn are applying for admission.

They proved it by spitting up on me after a nighttime feeding. The next morning, I attended the aforementioned birthday party with Xavier and Katie in a T-shirt streaked with spit-up stains.

But I didn't care. Meeting my newest grandchildren was a twin-win situation.

"The Kindest Cut of All"

In this age of rampant egotism and false pride, it's nice to know that there is still a genuine star who hasn't let fame go to his head, even after his head has just had a haircut.

I refer, of course, to Xavier. I also refer to Diego D'Ambrosio, who owns the barbershop where Xavier goes for a haircut but not, as yet, a shave, since he's only a toddler.

Still, Xavier and Diego stand head and shoulders above all the other notables in Washington, D.C., where I saw both stars.

I spent a week helping Katie and Dave with Zoe and Quinn, who needed to be fed, burped, changed, and brought to the doctor's office. I also helped with Xavier, who needed to be brought to school, played with afterward, read to before bed, and, on the last full day of my visit, taken for a haircut.

I found out when Katie and I walked into the doctor's office with Zoe and Quinn that Xavier isn't the only Xavier in the nation's capital.

"Xavier!" shouted a nurse.

"Xavier was here yesterday," Katie told me, looking confused. "He had a shot."

Just then, a young man with a child in his arms walked toward the back to see the doctor.

"There's another Xavier," I said. "But of course, he's not the main one. Our Xavier is."

"That's right," Katie said as she held Zoe, who promptly threw up all over the front of her mother's striped dress.

In the examination room, the doctor looked at the glistening streak and said, "It's like modern art."

Zoe and Quinn each had two shots and an oral vaccine. Afterward, Katie and I took them to a bar. We each had a beer. The twins, making their first visit to such an establishment, had already consumed their bottles (of milk) and were passed out in their two-seat stroller.

"It's good to get out of the house," Katie said.

"Cheers!" I replied, clinking glasses with her.

At the end of the week, Katie and I took Xavier to Diego's Hair Salon, which is on Diego D'Ambrosio Way.

"Diego must be the only barber in America who has a street named after him," I told Katie.

"He's famous," she said.

That was evident when we walked in and saw that the walls were lined with autographed photos of D.C. notables, among them Presidents Bill Clinton, George W. Bush, Barack Obama, and Donald Trump.

We had to wait for Xavier's turn, so we went back outside and encountered yet another Xavier, also a toddler and also waiting for a haircut.

"He's the second other Xavier we've met this week," I said to the second other Xavier's parents.

Back inside, Diego couldn't give Xavier a haircut because he had broken his hip and was using a walker, so Tania had the honor of cutting Xavier's hair. She did a wonderful job.

On the way out, I spoke with Diego, who is eighty-three and has owned his shop for more than half a century.

"You're famous," I told him.

Diego smiled modestly.

"My grandson is famous, too," I said. "He's been the star of many of my columns. I think you should have a photo of him on the wall. He'll even autograph it. In crayon."

"I'll put it up," Diego promised.

"And don't worry," I said. "Like you, Xavier won't let fame go to his handsome head."

CHAPTER 3

(My ever-growing to-do list has made me listless. But a man's got to do what he's got to do — especially if he's retired and his wife is still working and she wants him to be useful. Believe me, it's a chore.)

"A Long Bout of Social Insecurity"

When I turned sixty-five, the age at which I retired, I went to my local Social Security office to sign up for Medicare and encountered so many people that I figured I'd still be there when I turned sixty-six, at which time I could get full benefits.

"You can die of old age in this place," I said to a nice couple named Janice and Andrew, who sat next to me in the back row.

"Medicare won't cover it," said Janice, who's sixty-nine and still works as a school secretary.

"And if you're dead," added Andrew, sixty-six, who lost his job as a machinist, "you can't get Social Security anymore."

"It pays to stay alive," Janice said.

"If you can call this living," added Andrew, noting that it was the third time he and Janice had been in the Social Security office.

"This is my first time," I told them.

"You always remember your first time," Janice said with a wink.

I figured my visit would be unforgettable when I arrived at ten a.m. and walked into what looked like a Cecil B. DeMille epic.

"I've been here since 8:41," said Harry, fifty, who sat on my other side. He used crutches because he had leg surgery and was on temporary disability.

"What's your number?" I asked.

"D606," he said.

"Mine is A228," I told him.

"You'll probably get called before I do," said Harry. "They won't take pity on me."

"You're just using that as a crutch," I said.

Harry got up and limped away. He returned about five minutes later.

"Was it something I said?" I wondered.

Harry shook his head and replied, "I had to go to the bathroom."

In less time than it would take a kindergartner to read "War and Peace," my number was called.

"Bye, everybody!" I said and walked up to, appropriately, Window 0, behind which was a nice young woman who asked why I was there.

I told her I wanted to apply for Medicare, adding: "I would get COBRA, but I'd be covered only if I was bitten by a poisonous snake."

"May I have your Social Security number?" the woman asked.

I didn't want to yell it out in a place containing the approximate population of Luxembourg, so I wrote it on a piece of paper and slipped it under the window.

"You can sit down until you're called again," she said pleasantly.

When I returned to my seat, Janice, Andrew, and Harry said in unison, "Welcome back, Jerry!"

I scanned the room. Some people were on their phones, others were chatting, one woman was reading a book (not one of mine, unfortunately), and a fellow geezer was snoozing.

Another guy was wearing a sweatshirt with the skull-and-horns logo of the heavy metal band Five Finger Death Punch, which prompted Janice to say, "I'd like to give this place a one finger death punch."

Actually, it wasn't that bad. The Social Security folks were courteous and helpful. And the people I sat with, despite their grumbling, were friendly and funny.

"If you don't laugh," Janice remarked, "you'll cry."

I cried for joy when my name was called. I went to Window 1 and was told by another nice young woman that the earliest appointment was in two months.

"See you then," Janice said as I left. "We'll still be here."

"Moving Violations"

The best thing about being a baby boomer, aside from believing that sixty-five is the new forty-five, which explains why I can't balance my checkbook, is that you can still do everything you have always done, but if there is something you don't want to do anymore, you can pull the age card.

Lugging furniture falls into this category. If you are the lugger, you will fall, too, wrenching your back in the process.

That is why the Zezima Moving, Storage & Hernia Company is going out of business. I will say for legal purposes that the corporation is liquidating. The liquid, I hasten to add, is beer, which is what I have needed after each of the many moves I have made for family and friends over a painful period dating back to the Carter administration.

The last one occurred when I was assigned to remove a couch from my mother-in-law's house in Stamford, load it into a rented truck, and drive it to Long Island, where it had to be unloaded and replaced by another couch that then had to be driven to the landfill, where I also would have ended up if I could afford the dumping fee.

There were three main problems:

(a) My mother-in-law's couch weighed approximately as much as the truck.
(b) The house was evidently built around it.
(c) It was raining so hard that I should have rented an ark.

This required brains and brawn. Since I am sorely lacking in both, and have the soreness to prove it, I enlisted the help of my nephew Blair, who has a prodigious quantity of each, plus something I haven't had in the forty years since I was his age:

(d) Youth.

As the rain rained down, I had a brainstorm: I covered the couch with a drop cloth to protect it from the downpour. Unfortunately, the cloth was not waterproof. It was like putting a napkin on your head before walking under Niagara Falls.

To compound matters, the couch was leather. I know what you're thinking: Isn't leather kinky? Answer: Yes, which is why I got a massive kink in my back.

Leather is also slippery, which makes it hard to grasp, so I had to bend down and lift one end. Suddenly, a bolt of lightning coursed down my spine and stopped directly above my end.

Then Blair and I had to tilt the couch this way and that to get it through the narrow doorway and were instantly drenched by the monsoon outside.

With the aid of Sue and Lauren, we got the couch down a walkway, over a wall, and into the truck. I drove back in the pathetic vehicle, whose original owners must have been the Flintstones, and headed to Lauren's house.

There Guillaume and I risked further back trouble (he already had sciatica) by carrying the couch up a flight of stairs. We looked like Laurel and Hardy doing the same thing with a piano in "The Music Box," for which they won an Oscar.

Guillaume and I deserved a Harry because we were harried by our wives to get the couch into the house, from which we had to remove another couch, which thank God was lighter, and drive it to the dump.

"I'm too old for this," I told Sue after we had returned the truck and got into my car for the ride home. "The next time furniture needs to be lugged, someone else can do it."

Later, I settled my sore back onto our couch, which isn't going anywhere, and had a beer. It was the best move of the day.

"Those Are the Brakes"

Here is today's safe driving question:

If you are approaching the stop sign in front of my house, do you: (a) stop, (b) slow down to the posted speed limit, look to see if a cop is parked on the corner, and breeze past, or (c) pretend you are at the finish line in the Indianapolis 500 and blow right through?

If you answered either (b) or (c), you are part of the vast majority of vehicular maniacs who menace my neighborhood and deserve not only to get a ticket but to have the accelerator shoved up your nose.

You also should take an online refresher course so you will be a better driver and, ideally, not obliterate my car as I am backing out of the driveway.

I am proud, happy, and really fatigued to say that I took a six-hour safe driving course sponsored by AARP, which wants older motorists such as yours truly to be more aware of the rules of the road, to compensate for diminished physical and mental skills, and — this is most important — to stop driving twenty miles per hour in the left lane of a highway with their blinkers on.

As a person who always puts safety first, I took the course for a vital and selfless reason: to get a discount on my car insurance.

After logging in to the AARP Smart Driver Online Course and paying the twenty-five-dollar fee, I was introduced to two nice instructors named Joe and Maria, who would be guiding me through the class and giving me quizzes at the end of the half-dozen sections.

It was like taking driver's ed in high school except that I didn't actually have to drive and give the teacher a heart attack while accidentally flooring it and jumping the curb as I pulled out of the parking lot.

The first thing I learned is that I probably should let somebody else drive. That's because I am sixty-five years old and, according to Joe and Maria, who look to be forty-five, no longer have the reflexes, dexterity, and keen eyesight of twenty-five-year-olds. I must admit that they are far better equipped to speed, weave in and out of traffic, run red lights, and give one-finger salutes while texting, playing video games, drinking steaming hot coffee, or — and this takes special skill — applying eyeliner.

Maybe they shouldn't be driving, either.

But I was encouraged because Joe and Maria told me that I could sharpen my skills and continue to be a safe driver if I remembered the valuable lessons taught in the course. They included approaching intersections, merging into traffic, knowing the effects of prescription medication, preparing for trips, and checking the tires, though not while the car is moving.

In extreme circumstances, they strongly implied, I should just pull over and get the hell out of the way.

Joe and Maria have never driven with me, but I appreciated their confidence.

It turned out that I still know a lot about safe driving because I aced all the quizzes. And I picked up some important tips, like avoiding drivers who are going either too fast or too slow. Joe and Maria didn't state the obvious, but that includes everybody else.

Nonetheless, I am glad I took the course, which I did over several evenings. I would encourage all drivers of AARP age to take it, too.

In fact, now that I have graduated, motor cum laude, I am volunteering to join Joe and Maria as an instructor.

If I could only get all those idiots to stop blowing through the stop sign in front of my house, I'd feel a lot safer.

"A Tale of Two Fridges"

One man's junk, as the saying goes, is not his wife's treasure. That's why she will tell him to haul it to the dump so there will be room for not one but two new refrigerators, which will keep his beer cold so he'll have the strength to get rid of all that junk.

That was the messy situation in which I found myself after our nineteen-year-old kitchen refrigerator conked out. The auxiliary fridge, which was in the garage and was twenty-one, making it legally old enough to consume my beer, was on life support. It was only a matter of time before it pulled the plug on itself.

So Sue and I had to purchase a pair of fridges and clear space for their delivery. This meant getting rid of the junk that had accumulated in the garage since we moved into our house in 1998.

It included boxes of old newspapers and other stuff belonging to me, boxes of old ornaments and other stuff belonging to Sue, and boxes of old clothes and other stuff belonging to Katie and Lauren, who moved out of the house during the administration of George W. Bush.

I loaded my SUV (shambles utility vehicle) and made three trips to the dump, where I met Chris, who manned the attendant booth.

"You have a lot of junk," he said.

"I also have gas," I told him through the open driver's-side window.

"You should take something for it," Chris said as he stepped back. "This place smells bad enough."

"No, I mean I have cans of old gasoline," I replied. "Where do they go?"

Chris pointed to a section behind the booth, then told me where to put my other stuff, such as paper, glass, paint, recyclables, clothing, metal, wood, and household garbage.

"I'm getting rid of all this junk to make room for two new refrigerators," I said. "My beer got warm, so I had to take drastic action."

Chris sympathized because he owned a bar for fifteen years and knows the importance of cold beer.

"My customers loved it," said Chris, adding that he used to feed them Spam fries, which were made with the maligned luncheon meat. "My customers didn't love them."

Chris told me that Spam is popular in Hawaii because GIs brought cans of it there during World War II.

"My wife and I honeymooned in Hawaii," I said.

"Did you have Spam?" he asked.

"No," I replied. "But I did have poi, which I washed down with Hawaiian beer."

In a box of random junk, I found a Spam can that had been turned into a piggy bank. It contained thirty-nine cents.

"Now my wife and I can afford to go back," I told Chris.

But first I had to return home and await delivery of the refrigerators.

Jose and Mario took out the old kitchen fridge and replaced it with the new one. They did the same with the old and new ones in the garage, which had been cleared for passage.

"Do these refrigerators come with beer?" I asked.

"No, but it would be a good idea," said Jose. "Sales would increase if refrigerators came with beer."

"I'd offer you some," I said, "but it's warm."

After Jose and Mario left, Sue stocked our two new fridges with food and I put in the beer, which was soon cold again.

I opened one and made a toast: "To running refrigerators and a clean garage. And a second honeymoon in Hawaii."

"First," Sue said, "we have to pay for the appliances."

"I have thirty-nine cents," I told her.

"Good," said Sue. "Buy yourself a can of Spam. It'll go great with your beer."

"Wrestling With Unmentionables"

It may be true that everything comes out in the wash, but it's also true that if you're in a laundromat, you shouldn't take off your bra in front of other customers before doing the wash.

That's the valuable lesson I learned after the dryer conked out and Sue, who has never, to my knowledge, removed her brassiere in public, dispatched me to the laundromat to finish a load of wet clothes.

"You see everything in this place," said manager Angel Lopez. "One night, a lady started getting undressed so she could put her clothes in the washer. She was topless and was just wearing her underwear. I went over to her and said, 'Really? You couldn't do this before you got here?'"

"Maybe," I suggested helpfully, "it was her only bra."

"Listen," Angel said, "men are just as bad. Like the guy last night who told me that if he didn't do the laundry right, his wife said he was a dead man. He said, 'Are you going to help me?' I said, 'No. I want to see if she's going to kill you.'"

"My wife is too nice to resort to murder over socks and bath towels," I said. "How about your wife?"

Angel smiled and replied, "I'm not married."

Not that he wouldn't be a good catch, even though he is widely considered a bad guy.

"In addition to working at the laundromat," Angel said, "I'm a professional wrestler."

He wrestles under the name of Cano Lopez, the Exorcist.

"Cano is my mother's maiden name," said Angel, who has "Cano" tattooed on his right forearm and "Lopez" on his left.

"In the ring, I'm a villain," he said. "People boo me, but between matches, kids come up to me and say, 'Can I have your autograph?'"

"Do you wrestle in the WWE?" I asked. "It's headquartered in my hometown of Stamford, Connecticut."

"I wish!" said Angel, who's affiliated with East Coast Pro Wrestling.

At fifty-three, he's one of the oldest wrestlers on the circuit. But at five-foot-eight and two hundred and twenty-seven pounds, he's one tough geezer.

"You have to be," said Angel. "We get hit with steel chairs, jump off buckles, and land on wooden boards. We're like actors who do our own stunts." He winced and added, "I'm fifty-three, but my body says eighty-three."

One of Angel's brothers, Marc Static, is a wrestler, too. They're two of twenty-four siblings, twelve brothers and twelve sisters. "I'm number seventeen," Angel said.

"There must have been a lot of laundry in your family," I noted.

"Mountains of it," Angel said. "It prepared me for my job here."

And he does it extremely well. In addition to being an amateur psychologist ("I listen to everybody's problems," he said), Angel is an appliance engineer, a lint expert, and a folding consultant.

"Did you know that a buildup of lint could cause a fire in the dryer?" he said.

"No," I answered. "Just to be safe, I'd better clean it out of my belly button, too."

After using one of the dryers without starting a three-alarm blaze, I asked Angel for help in folding the towels, socks, and underwear in my laundry basket.

"The towels go corner to corner, then fold them again, the long way, in a trifold," he instructed. "The edges go in the closet."

The opening of one sock in each pair is folded over the mate "so they won't become separated," Angel said. "And underwear is pretty easy. Now you try it."

I passed the folding test with all the flying colors of my towels, socks, and boxer shorts.

"Your wife will be impressed," said Angel.

"Next time I come here, I'll bring her," I replied. "And I promise she won't take off her bra."

"It All Comes Out in the Wash"

Because I don't do laundry, even though I often air it in public, I am frequently in hot water. But I didn't want my house to be in it, too, so I contracted to replace the water heater, which threatened to blow like Old Faithful and spray steaming hot water all over me, which at least would have allowed me to do laundry without having to take off my dirty socks and underwear.

The two guys who came over to do the job were the father-and-son team of Keith and Keith Scanlon.

Keith Sr., sixty-three, and Keith Jr., twenty-five, are hot stuff themselves.

"I hope he's a good cop," father said of son, who has applied for the NYPD, "because he's a terrible plumber."

Replied son, "Not all of us have been doing this since dinosaurs roamed the earth."

Even though Keith Sr. has been in the business for forty years, he's not exactly prehistoric, which is more than I could say for the oil burner, a rusty contraption that was in worse shape than the water heater and had turned the laundry room into the appliance version of Jurassic Park.

"It did its time," Keith Sr. declared.

"Are you going to put it out of its misery?" I asked.

"Yes," Keith Sr. answered, adding: "Now it's going to cause us some misery."

That's because the metal hulk weighed eight hundred and sixty pounds.

"Being a cop has to be easier than this," Keith Jr. said as he and his father loaded the burner onto a dolly, wheeled it through the garage, and put it on a device that lifted it into the back of their truck. "The heaviest lifting I'll have to do on the NYPD is bringing guys to jail."

"At least this keeps me in shape," said Keith Sr., who has no plans to retire because he has three adult children — Keith Jr. is the "baby" — and has to pay for weddings and help with college tuition bills.

"I was father of the bride recently," said Keith Sr., whose younger daughter, Arianna, had a destination wedding in Mexico.

"It was unbelievable," Keith Sr. said, adding that the groom, Aleck, had his bachelor party in Iceland. "I didn't go," Keith Sr. noted, "but my son-in-law's family is from Macedonia, so we're going to have a second event in the U.S. so they can attend."

I told Keith Sr. that I have been father of the bride to both of my daughters and that the younger one was married in France.

"We also had a second event in the U.S. for the people from here who couldn't make it there," I said.

"We have a lot in common," Keith Sr. said when I told him that my daughters took a trip to Iceland.

"I didn't go, either," I noted.

"My older daughter is named Lauren," he said.

"That's my younger daughter's name," I replied.

"My wife, Antoinette, and I have been married for thirty-nine years," Keith Sr. said.

"My wife, Sue, and I have been married for forty-one," I said, "but I'm two years older than you are, so it evens out."

Then I found out that Keith Sr. and Antoinette were married two days after my older daughter, Katie, was born.

"Do you do laundry?" I asked.

"No," Keith Sr. answered.

"Neither do I," I told him.

"We're so much alike, it's incredible," he said.

The one thing we don't have in common is that I'm retired.

"If you get in your wife's hair, you could work for me," Keith Sr. said. "Now that she has a new water heater, she won't mind washing your dirty socks and underwear."

CHAPTER 4

(If I have learned anything since being retired, it's that a man's home is his hassle. The man's wife, who runs the house, would agree. Fortunately, all the people needed for never-ending repairs are still working.)

"The Height of Folly"

Because I suffer from acrophobia, which is an irrational fear of being any higher off the ground than the top of my head, I would rather have a root canal while listening to a telemarketer than get up on the roof of my house, a two-story Colonial that could give a mountain goat nosebleeds.

But I got up there with a fearless young man who came over to give me an estimate for a new roof.

"I never realized I was petrified of heights until we bought this house and I had to clean the gutters every fall," I told Anthony Amini, who owns Performance Contracting and Management, the Long Island company that Sue and I were considering for the job. "Even the word 'fall' makes me nervous."

"You should have gotten gutter guards," Anthony said.

"I did," I replied. "Now I don't have to get up on the roof anymore."

"Except for today," said Anthony, who agreed to my frankly stupid request to accompany him on a trip atop the Mount Everest of houses.

As Anthony put a ladder against the family room extension, which at one story has the lowest of our three roofs, I asked, "Are you afraid of heights?"

"No," Anthony responded.

"Have you ever fallen off a roof?" I wanted to know.

"I'm here, aren't I?" he said.

"What's your secret?" I inquired.

"Don't look down," Anthony answered.

I didn't even want to look up. But I had to as I began my ascent, which took so long that it could have been timed with a sundial.

"This isn't so bad, is it?" Anthony said as I stood, knees shaking, next to our leaky skylight, which he said needed to be replaced.

"Skylights are great on sunny days," I told him, "but otherwise, they're floods waiting to happen."

Even though we were only about ten feet up, Anthony complimented me on my bravery after I was back on terra firma, a Latin term meaning "the place where you will be buried if you fall off the roof."

But the coward in me came out, in pathetic whimpers, when I had to climb to the top of the house. Remembering Anthony's admonition not to look down, I stared into a second-story window and saw my reflection, which bore a frightening resemblance to the Edvard Munch painting "The Scream," except with a mustache.

When I had reached the summit and surveyed my kingdom, which costs a king's ransom in property taxes, I exclaimed, "Look, it's the Great Wall of China!"

"That's your fence," Anthony noted.

He said our altitude was about thirty feet. It seemed like thirty-thousand feet. A plane flew past. I waved to the pilot.

"You're doing great," Anthony said as I stood stock-still, my feet straddling the crown of the roof, afraid to move. "You can join my crew. I'll have you carry up shingles."

"I may have to be carried down," I stammered.

Then I noticed that my right sneaker was untied. Anthony bent down to lace it up, making a double knot.

"I've done it for my kids," he said.

I slowly made my way back to the ladder and climbed down, only to climb up again, this time to the roof above the garage, kitchen, and laundry room, a mere eighteen feet high.

As he did on the other parts of the roof, Anthony took measurements and showed me what needed to be done.

Later, as Sue and I sat with Anthony in the kitchen, where he gave us a reasonable estimate, I said, "I just renewed my life insurance policy."

"Looks like I'll have to wait to collect," said Sue.

"Your husband is very courageous," Anthony told her.

"Coming from you," I said with a sigh of relief, "that's high praise."

"Painter's Helper Is Off the Wall"

According to a cherished old adage, which I know is true because I just made it up, if you can't stand the kitchen, turn up the heat.

That's what Sue did because she wanted me to take down the wallpaper that had adorned the kitchen for the past dozen years.

"It's practically new," I told her.

"It's old," Sue countered. "And ugly. I want it down."

The last time I tried to remove wallpaper, in an upstairs bedroom when Sue and I moved into our house, it came off in pieces the size of lollipop wrappers. It took me three days. I could have saved a lot of time by using a flamethrower.

Thanks to those haunting flashbacks, I convinced Sue to hire Mike the Paint Guy.

Mike, otherwise known as Michael Beck, turned out to be a good worker who was having a bad week.

The day he was supposed to start, he had to take his father to the hospital. Then he had a flat tire. Worst of all, he had a calcium deposit in his shoulder that required surgery.

"The doctor said I have the body of a sixty-four-year-old man," said Michael, who is thirty-two.

"I'm more than twice your age," I told him. "My body is nothing to write home about, and neither is my head, but at least I don't need surgery."

"Maybe," Michael said, "you can help me take down the wallpaper."

"Sure," I said. "I'm off the wall myself, so I'd be happy to assist."

As Michael prepped the walls with a solution to make the paper come off easily, he asked, "What solution did you use when you took down the wallpaper upstairs?"

My response: "Beer."

"Wallpaper is tricky," Michael said. "Nobody uses it anymore. I've taken a lot of wallpaper down, but I haven't put any up."

When he got it down in the kitchen, he said, "Now I have to spackle. It will cover up the holes."

"Spackle is also good for covering up wrinkles," I noted. "I put it on my face before I go to bed."

"You do look young," Michael said, "so I guess it works."

Next, he revved up an electric sander to smooth out the walls.

"May I try?" I asked.

"Help yourself," Michael said as he handed me the whirring disc.

"This thing could give me a close shave," I said.

"Yes," said Michael, "but then you'd need more spackle to cover up the nicks and cuts."

On one of the walls was a phone number. It was for a woman named Bernice, which also was the name of one of our deceased cats. I called, but the number was out of service.

"It's dead, too," I told Michael.

Now it was time to paint. Michael's shoulder was bothering him, so I said, "You'll have a brush with disaster. Let me help."

As I did one of the walls, I remarked, "I'm on a roll!"

It caused Michael even more pain. But he worked through it and, almost single-handedly over the course of a week, and despite my feeble assistance, did a fantastic job.

"I love it!" Sue exclaimed. "Now I want the hallway painted."

"You'll have to wait until Michael is out of surgery," I said.

"Then you can do the prep work," she said.

"OK," I replied. "Buy some spackle and an electric sander. And don't forget the beer."

"An Old Goof Has a New Roof"

For years, people have said I am all wet, even during droughts, so I wasn't surprised that until recently, my house was all wet, too.

That's because there was water, water everywhere and, since I ran out of beer, not a drop to drink.

Water was coming in through the ceiling, through a skylight, and even through a kitchen cabinet. It was enough to make me go through the roof, which not only would have made the situation worse but might have given me a concussion, not that anyone could tell the difference.

So Sue told me to call the insurance company.

"I hope we have an umbrella policy," I said.

Sue ignored the remark and said, "I want to see if the roof is covered."

"It's not covered," I replied. "That's why we have a water problem."

"You're going to have a problem," said Sue, who specifically mentioned how she could benefit from cashing in my life insurance policy.

Two days later, an adjuster named Doug came over to survey the damage.

"Do you think the value of the house would increase if I had an indoor swimming pool?" I asked.

"It might," Doug said. "You could bring in some sand and beach chairs."

"Would the insurance company pay for it?" I wondered.

"No," said Doug, adding that he has seen far worse situations. "In one case, the entire first floor was under water," he recalled. "Cars have driven through houses. We've covered the damage. There was even a lady who spilled bleach on her carpet. We replaced it."

"If I want a new carpet," I said, "should I spill bleach on it?"

"You can try," said Doug, "but I won't be your adjuster."

He did, however, send us a check and suggested we call a general contractor.

Anthony Amini was the man for the job.

"He was a great war hero," I told Anthony. "Killed at Gettysburg."

"Who?" Anthony asked.

"General Contractor," I said.

Anthony saluted and sized up the situation.

"Your roof is old," he said. "It's outdated and worn out."

"Sounds like me," I responded.

"My roof was the same," said Anthony. "I had a leaky skylight, just like you. When it rained, I had to put a bucket underneath it."

"My wife wanted me to put a new roof on my bucket list," I said.

"So did mine," Anthony told me. "She said, 'You do two or three roofs a week. Do this one.' I said, 'OK, babe.' Now we have a brand-new roof."

"I bet you know a good roofer," I said.

"I do," said Anthony. "He's a very nice guy and a very handsome guy. And he did a great job."

It was the same kind of job he did on our roof. And, with a hardworking crew of eight guys, it was done in one day.

"You had some issues in the valleys," Anthony told me.

"How about the mountains?" I asked.

"There, too," he said, adding that he gave me new boots.

"I could have worn them when the ceiling leaked," I said.

"You also got new gooseneck vents," Anthony said. "One of the old ones had a hairline fracture."

"I should have called a doctor," I said.

"It wouldn't have been covered under your medical plan," said Anthony, who also put in new ice and water shields and replaced the skylight in the family room.

"Things are looking up," I said, looking up at my beautiful new roof.

"It's guaranteed for twenty years," Anthony said, "but it should last for thirty or forty."

"I probably won't be around then," I said. "But since the ceiling doesn't leak anymore, I can kick the bucket now."

"This Electrician Is a Live Wire"

I have always been considered a dim bulb, except for the fact that I married a bright woman, who proves it by making me the one to risk electrocution whenever a light bulb needs to be changed.

So fearful am I when it comes to wattage that I was shocked — shocked! — to find myself helping out with electrical work being done at our house.

The track lighting in the family room had to be dismantled and replaced with high hats. And the ceiling fan and the chandelier in the kitchen both had to be updated. Because I could never perform these tasks without turning myself into a lightning rod, I hired Ed Knopf, a licensed electrician who, against his better judgment, made me his apprentice for the day.

"Do you know anything about electricity?" Ed asked.

"Of course," I replied. "How do you think my hair got so curly?"

In his forty years in the business, Ed has gotten a jolt or two himself. He said, "You have to watch out for live wires."

That includes hot women.

"I've had a few who were scantily dressed and were coming on to me," Ed said.

"Did they want to make sparks fly?" I asked.

"I guess so," he said. "Nothing happened because I was married at the time. But I did make sparks fly for a guy who wouldn't leave me alone. He was standing right next to me to see what I was doing."

"Was he making you hot under the collar?" I inquired.

"He was burning me up," Ed said. "So I shorted out the wires on purpose. Sparks flew and he was gone. I had to reset the circuit breakers, but it was worth it."

I'm not sure it was worth it to have me as an apprentice, but I tried to help.

"Here," Ed said as he stood on a ladder and handed me the track lighting. "You have to do something. You can't just stand there and look pretty."

I looked plastered when plaster fell on my head while Ed cut holes in the ceiling so he could run wires through. After handing me a handful of screws, he said, "Don't screw up."

I handed Ed the high hats and listened as he told me about more wacky customers.

"At this one house, the power was off and the homeowner wanted to turn the lights on," he said. "I told her I would get shocked. Then I said, 'Don't you know electricians can see in the dark?' She said, 'They can?' She wasn't too bright herself."

Then there was the guy who thought Ed and his then-girlfriend, who was helping him install a fan, were having sex in the attic.

"It was ninety degrees and we were up there for a while," Ed said. "But we were just working. Honest."

The worst customers are the ones who try to do electrical work themselves.

"I'm surprised they don't burn their houses down," said Ed, adding: "My favorite line is: 'I have no idea where these wires go.' I always say that to people."

As he was installing the new ceiling fan in the kitchen, he said, "I was working with a friend once and he said, 'Quiet, can't you see I'm thinking?' I said, 'I thought I smelled something burning.' The woman who owned the house said, 'Burning? What's burning?' She panicked. I said, 'Lady, that's a figure of speech.' You run into some real doozies in this job."

The biggest doozy, I'm sure, was me. But at least I made myself useful and didn't turn on the power before Ed was finished.

"You did a good job," he said. "Your wife will be happy to know that you're not so dim after all."

"Home, Sweat Home"

In all the years Sue and I have owned our house, we have had an open-door policy: Whenever work needs to be done, we open our door to a variety of handymen, licensed professionals, and other skilled workers who can do what I can't, which is practically everything.

As the Least Handy Man in America, even I knew that we should have installed a revolving door (which would have required the services of yet another laborer) because so many things needed fixing that our humble abode looked like the set of a Hollywood blockbuster.

The cast included Anthony the Contractor, Chris the Carpenter and Painter, Mario the Spackler, Andy the Plumber, Ed the Electrician, and Luis, Don, and Richard the Boiler Boys.

The work included ripping up the family room carpet, installing a vinyl floor, spackling the ceiling, and then painting it, all of which needed to be done because of water damage that also ruined a kitchen cabinet, which had to be removed, as did part of the soffit above the sink. The empty space, which contained traces of mold, had to be cleaned before a new corner cabinet, which was tough to find, could be installed.

Then there were plumbing and electrical issues involving a bleeder valve in an upstairs bedroom (the water leaked down to the kitchen) and the conking out of the downstairs thermostat, which made the house feel like a sauna, then turned the whole damn place into an ice box, which was appropriate since we had to pay for everything in cold cash.

"The Money Pit" had nothing on us. As I told Sue in the midst of all this craziness, "Home is where the heart attack is."

But it was actually fun. And all the guys were great. So was their workmanship.

Every morning, Anthony and Chris (and sometimes Mario or Andy) would come over for a day of hard work, which couldn't begin until Sue and I gave them breakfast. On the menu were coffee, bagels, and doughnuts. Butter, cream cheese, milk, and sugar also were available.

"Service with a smile!" Sue chirped.

"I'd make eggs," I said, "but I'm afraid I would burn the house down."

"Even we couldn't fix that," said Anthony.

The guys would work until lunch. I am always out to lunch, but on these days I stayed in. Sometimes Anthony and Chris went out, too, but on other days they also stayed in. I ordered pizza a couple of times and once Sue served corned beef sandwiches. There were homemade cookies for dessert.

"You're making us fat," Anthony said.

"Growing boys need their nourishment," Sue told them.

"Besides," I added, "you're really working it off."

One day, the work started at 7:30 in the morning, when Mario came over to spackle, and ended at 7:30 at night, when Don came over to check out the thermostat. (Long story short: We had to order a new one. In the meantime, we froze our assets off.)

Another day, Jason and Mike the Pest Control Guys came over but stayed outside when I told them I was the pest inside.

"I don't think we could control you," Jason said.

After Andy fixed our plumbing problem, Sue said, "We'll call you if we have any more cracks."

I pointed to my head, which prompted Andy to say, "I don't think I could fix that one."

When Ed, who had done great electrical work for us before, came back to check out some wires, Sue said, "Let's have a party!"

For two weeks, it was a party every day. But all good, noisy, dusty things must come to an end.

"I miss them," Sue said when Anthony and Chris left.

"They'll be back," I replied. "A house is not a home unless there's something to do."

"A Fence Goes From Holey to Heavenly"

Good fences, as every homeowner knows, make bad property taxes. Bad fences make trouble, unless you have good neighbors, who are a blessing when a fence needs to be replaced.

And, lo, I was blessed not only with good neighbors, but with the fence guy for the pope.

Chris Curcio installed the fence around St. Patrick's Cathedral in New York City when Pope Francis came to town in 2015.

"Did you meet the pope?" I asked Chris when he and his assistant, J.B. Becak, arrived to replace my backyard fence.

"No, but I saw him drive by," said Chris. "He waved and gave me a blessing."

"I've never met the pope, either," I said. "But a cardinal lives in one of our trees."

Chris told me that his full name is Christian.

"Does the pope know that?" I asked.

"I don't think so," Chris said. "But I hope it helps."

"Have you ever been the fence guy for any other celebrities?" I wondered.

"Yes," Chris replied. "I got the job when Trump and Hillary Clinton debated at Hofstra University in 2016."

"Where do I rank among your customers?" I wanted to know.

"You're just below the pope," said Chris, "but way above the politicians."

It was a great compliment considering that Chris, who's sixty and owns Long Island-based Complete Fence and Railing, has had countless customers in his forty years in the business.

"You know who a fence guy's best friend is?" Chris said.

"Who?" I responded.

"A nosy neighbor," he answered. "It will make somebody say, 'I need a fence.' There's the old saying, 'Good fences make good neighbors.' But bad neighbors are good for me."

"Do you have good neighbors?" I asked Chris, who has a four-foot-tall chain link fence bordering his property.

"Not the one who lives to the right of my house," he said. "She's getting a six-foot privacy fence. And I'm going to install it."

As Chris has learned over the years, installation can lead to confrontation.

"On one job, there was a corner post and four people were involved," he recalled. "They were fighting over where I was putting it. I said, 'Leave me alone.' People fight over inches. I've put up fences where I couldn't step on the neighbor's property."

Nonetheless, people aren't the greatest challenge.

"You know the number-one enemy of fence guys?" Chris said.

"What?" I replied.

"Lawn sprinklers. We bust them for a living," he said, adding: "I saw your sprinklers. They're safe."

Unfortunately, our old fence wasn't. It had holes big enough for dogs and cats to come through. One spot could have accommodated a grizzly bear.

So I asked my good backyard neighbor, Ann Marie, who had put up the fence many years before, if she wanted to split a new one, though not a fence of the split rail variety. Her good next-door neighbor, Leo, was replacing his perfectly usable stockade fence, which bordered the backyard of my good next-door neighbor, Bob, with a PVC fence.

Ann Marie kindly agreed and we got a great price from Chris, who is also the fence guy for Leo.

Chris and J.B., who both look like Olympic weightlifters, dismantled the old fence with tools and muscle.

"It's good exercise," said J.B., forty-seven, who also owns J.B. 24-Hour Towing Service.

"My truck broke down the other day," he told me. "I had to call another towing company. They double-charged me."

Chris and J.B. attached the stockade fence to several posts, none of which was The Washington Post or the New York Post, and the improvement was remarkable.

"Now grizzly bears can't get through," Chris said.

"Great job," I told him. "This is the answer to my prayers."

"When you're the fence guy for the pope," Chris said, "miracles do happen."

CHAPTER 5

(When you're retired, lots of crazy things happen to make life more interesting. You can be anywhere — on the ground, in the air, or even in a store that sells lingerie. Here are the revealing details.)

"Dot's the Car for Poppie"

If a car dealership is looking for someone to star in its TV commercials, a funny, smart, trusted spokesperson who is an expert in style and the best color for your new vehicle, I have the perfect candidate.

I refer, of course, to Chloe.

Chloe, who has a lifetime of experience with crayons, has two favorite colors: blue and pink. Those are my favorite colors, too, because Chloe has told me they are.

So when I called her to say I was going to look for a new car, I asked what color I should get.

"Get blue, Poppie," Chloe advised.

"How about pink?" I wondered.

"No," Chloe said. "Get blue. With pink polka dots."

That afternoon, Sue and I went to Hyundai 112 and saw James Boyd, a super salesman who is starring in a TV commercial for the Long Island dealership.

"You're a celebrity," I told him.

"I haven't seen the commercial yet," said James, who asked what I was looking for in a new car.

"Brakes," I replied. "They're pretty important. And wheels. An engine would help, too."

"I can do that," he said. "I can also get you all the bells and whistles."

"If I wanted bells and whistles," I said, "I'd buy a train."

James said I could trade in my old Santa Fe for a new one, but that it wouldn't be keyless.

"Even keyless cars need keys," I pointed out.

"That's a key point," James responded with a straight face. "But the car doesn't come with seat warmers."

"I already have them," I said. "They're called pants."

When Sue and I returned from a test drive, James asked how we liked the car. I shrugged and replied, "The cop said the accident wasn't my fault."

He blanched. Sue shook her head and said, "Ignore him."

But James, thirty-nine, a charming guy who has been in the business for eighteen years, couldn't ignore the fact that we wanted to buy the car. He got us an excellent deal.

After checking out my old white car, James said, "You have the best vanity plates I have ever seen."

The plates — JZEE — were Sue's idea.

"It took me months to get them," she told James.

"What do you think the real Jay-Z would say?" James wondered.

"I'm the real one," I said. "I'm older than he is and I had the name first. And my wife is even more beautiful than his."

Sue blushed. Then she said, "We have to pick a color."

"Our granddaughter wants me to get blue," I told James.

"I can do that," he said.

"With pink polka dots," I added.

"Anything for you, JZEE," he promised. "But you may have to buy a paintball gun."

James said that the available shade of blue was called Stormy Sea.

"Better than Stormy Daniels," I noted.

Sue agreed.

When the transaction was done, I asked the celebrity salesman for his autograph. James took out a pen and, on a sheet of paper, signed, "To JZEE: Best wishes. Drive safely!! James T. Boyd"

"Now I want yours," he said.

"I already gave you about forty-seven autographs on the paperwork," I said.

After we all shook hands, Sue and I drove home, where I called Chloe.

"I got a new car," I told her.

"Wow!" she said. "What color?"

"Blue."

"With pink polka dots?"

"No," I confessed.

"You have to get pink polka dots, Poppie."

James was right: I may have to buy a paintball gun.

"With Beer, the Sky's the Limit"

Every time I hear that somebody is on cloud nine, I wonder what happened to the first eight clouds. But the ninth altocumulus, not to be confused with the second alto sax, was where I found myself after the airplane on which I was a passenger had to turn back, possibly after hitting the fourth altostratus, causing so much inconvenience that I got a free beer out of the deal.

My anxious airplane adventure began en route to Washington, D.C., where I was winging it, solo, to visit Katie, Dave, Xavier, Zoe, and Quinn.

About ten minutes into the ten a.m. flight from New York's LaGuardia Airport, where it takes longer to find a parking space than it does to fly to Washington, something felt wrong. It was as if the engine was wired on caffeine and couldn't stop humming a really bad song that plays over and over in your head.

My head, which had been empty, filled with dread as I saw Shaqwanna, one of the two flight attendants, on the phone. As soon as she hung up, I heard this announcement: "Due to a mechanical issue, we are returning to LaGuardia. Please fasten your seatbelts."

There was, we were informed, a problem with the bleed line.

"Sounds like the plane needs a transfusion," I told Toni, the very nice retired woman sitting next to me.

"Are you a doctor?" she asked.

"No," I replied, my heart racing, "but I could use one."

The bleed line, we were further informed, provides air that pressurizes the cabin. It would take about fifteen minutes to fix once we were back at LaGuardia. If that didn't work, we'd have to change planes.

"To make up for this," I asked Paige, the other flight attendant, "will you be serving beer?"

"It's always an option," replied Paige, who had been on the job for only two months. "I've had some delays," she told me, "but this is the first time we've had to turn around."

After we landed, I spoke with the pilot, a pleasant young man named Joe, who looked barely old enough to drive a car, let alone fly a plane.

"Do I qualify for infrequent flier miles?" I inquired.

"Considering we didn't go too far, you should," said Joe, who has been flying for six years.

"Paige told me I could get a free beer," I said.

"She's the boss," Joe stated.

It turned out that the problem had no quick fix, so we had to change planes. We got off and were directed to a terminal gate where our new plane would be.

On a table, there were snacks, which served as the lunch we would not be served once we were again airborne.

I walked up to the desk and spoke with a friendly "customer experience representative" named Yvette.

"I was told by the crew that I could get a free beer," I said.

"You deserve one," Yvette said with a smile. Then she handed me a voucher for a complimentary cocktail.

About half an hour later, we boarded the new plane. I took my seat and, after taking off, waited for Paige to come by with the refreshment cart.

"Hello!" she chirped. "Welcome back!"

"I have a voucher for that free beer," I said.

"Here you go," said Paige, handing me a cold one.

Later, I handed her my drained can.

"This really hit the spot," I said.

"I'm glad," said Paige.

I was glad the new plane didn't have to turn around.

After we landed in D.C., I congratulated Joe on a good flight.

"The second time's the charm," he noted.

"I was on cloud nine," I said. "And I got here on a wing and a beer."

"Bellying Up to the Genius Bar"

If this column is being read by Apple CEO Tim Cook, known to a certain ubiquitous Twitter user as Tim Apple, it means two things:

1. He has way too much time on his hands.
2. He should acknowledge that I am a genius.

I attained this lofty status after I bought a new iMac and enlisted the services of Yash Sharma, who works in a nearby Apple store.

I went there because my previous iMac was ten years old, slower than a tortoise with a broken leg, and the technological equivalent of me: a geezer.

I took the new computer home and called Apple Support for help in setting it up because I was afraid I would plug it into the wrong outlet, hit "Control-Alt-Delete," and bring down the nation's power grid.

Everything was fine except for the unfortunate fact that I couldn't transfer data from my old computer to my new one. So I had to take both machines to the store.

"Do you have an external hard drive?" Yash asked.

"I have a hard drive, but it's not external," I said. "I didn't want to put it outside. What if it rains?"

This, of course, was before I became a genius.

At twenty-one, Yash has already achieved that designation, which qualifies him to help customers like me who otherwise would have to rely on their grandchildren for technical assistance.

"Sometimes with older computers, you have to reboot," said Yash.

"My definition of rebooting," I told him, "is to put your foot through the screen. Before I retired, we had a new computer system at work and the best thing I could say about it is that it made the old one look good. Still," I added, "I don't think anybody ever ran through an office yelling, 'The typewriters are down!'"

"Probably not," Yash said. "So it's a good thing you came to the Genius Bar."

"Do you serve beer at this bar?" I asked.

"We don't have a liquor license," Yash replied.

"That's too bad," I said. "Since you're twenty-one, you could have a cold one with me."

"After your computer problem is fixed," he said, "you could go to another bar and celebrate."

That was easier said than done because even Yash had trouble transferring the data, so he had to bypass the hard drive and hook both computers to each other so my information could go directly from the old one to the new one.

"This could take a while," he told me.

The estimated time for completion was eight hours and forty-nine minutes. The store closed in about an hour.

"You'll have to leave them here overnight," Yash said.

"It'll be like a hospital stay," I noted. "My machines will have a double room in the ICU: Intensive Computer Unit."

"It usually costs ninety-nine dollars for this," Yash said, "but we won't charge you because you've already done ninety-nine dollars' worth of work yourself."

"I'm sixty-five years old and I haven't done ninety-nine dollars' worth of work in my whole life," I said. "But thanks."

I received a call the next morning to say that the operation was a success. When I picked up the computers, I said to Yash, "I've learned a lot from you. In fact, I feel like a genius."

"Maybe you could work here," he suggested.

"Tell that to Tim Cook," I said. "And tell him to start serving beer at the Genius Bar. The first round is on him."

"A Real Wake-up Call"

I am not easily alarmed, except when I look in the mirror to shave, but my house is. That's because the alarm keeps blaring. According to Judy, who works for the alarm company, the reason is simple:

The house is haunted.

"What other explanation can there be?" Judy asked after she called me at one a.m. on a stormy night. The call woke me out of a sound sleep in which I dreamed that the alarm was blaring.

Actually, it was, as Judy helpfully pointed out when I picked up the phone.

"I can't hear you," I told her. "The alarm is blaring."

"Turn it off," Judy politely instructed me.

"What?" I said.

"TURN IT OFF!" yelled Judy, whose ears must have been ringing even more than mine.

I went to the keypad in the kitchen and punched in the security code, which in my semiconscious state I temporarily forgot (when you have one hundred and forty-seven different passwords for various things, it's tough to keep track).

After the alarm stopped blaring and my hearing was restored, I told Judy about the storm.

"Do you have a lot of wind?" she asked.

"I did after dinner," I responded, "but I'm feeling much better now."

"The problem is coming from Zone 12," Judy reported.

"I'm usually in the Twilight Zone," I said.

"Is that where you are now?" Judy asked.

"Yes," I said. "It's the family room."

"Check the slider," she said.

"We have French doors," I told her. "And I don't even speak French."

"Is the door ajar?" Judy inquired.

It was all I could do to keep from making another stupid joke, so I checked it and said, "Yes."

"Do you want me to call the police?" Judy asked.

"No," I said. "I don't want to go back to prison."

"You were in prison?" Judy spluttered.

"Yes," I replied honestly. "Rikers Island."

"For how long?" she wanted to know.

"About six hours," I responded, explaining that I was there several years ago to talk about writing to young detainees who were in school at the maximum-security facility. "My columns are criminal," I added, "but I was paroled anyway. I must have been a bad influence on the inmates."

"If nobody forced the door open," Judy theorized, "it was probably the wind."

"This isn't the first time it's happened," I said. "We've gotten calls from the alarm company about the motion sensor in the living room."

"That's Zone 10," Judy said. "Did anybody break in?"

"No," I said. "The person who called the last time said it could have been the plants on the windowsill. It was during the day and I was out, so I had to rush home to see what was going on."

"What was going on?" Judy wondered.

"I guess the plants were having a party," I said.

"Maybe they needed to be watered," Judy guessed.

"They were probably headed for the liquor cabinet in the dining room," I said.

"That's Zone 8," Judy told me.

"Why does this keep happening?" I asked.

"There's only one logical explanation," Judy said. "Your house is haunted."

"That would explain the spirits in the liquor cabinet," I noted.

"Or," Judy said, "your sensor in very sensitive."

"It must have heard the bad things I've called it after the alarm has gone off so many times," I said.

"Make sure all your doors and windows are tightly closed," Judy said.

"Thank you," I said. "You've been very helpful. I'm sorry you have to work so late, but I'm glad you're alert."

"That's my job," said Judy. "Have a good rest of the night."

"You, too," I said.

"Now," Judy said, "you can sleep easier."

"I will," I said with a yawn. "Unless the alarm starts blaring again."

"This Cold Was Something to Sneeze At"

When it comes to being sick, men are babies. I know this because there are six children in my family (five grandkids and yours truly) and I was sicker than any of them over a period of five months, which is how long it took me to recover from an illness that so baffled medical science that it was impervious to prescription medication and was finally eradicated with a self-prescribed dose of blackberry brandy.

It all started after Zoe and Quinn were born. Before Sue and I took a trip to meet them, I had a flu shot. The pharmacist who gave it to me said I was very brave considering that many men are — you guessed it — babies when it comes to needles.

"Some of them have even fainted," she said.

"Wimps," I replied as I rolled up my sleeve. "I'm ready for my shot now."

"I just gave it to you," the pharmacist said as she put a Band-Aid on my arm. "Stay healthy!"

I wish I could say I did, but I came down with something I thought was either the flu or a sinus infection or black lung disease. So I walked into a walk-in clinic to make sure I wasn't contagious.

"You're not," said a physician, who took a throat culture with a swab that was attached to a stick approximately the length of a javelin.

"Do I have a pulse?" I inquired.

"Yes," he reported. "You are, technically, still alive. And the culture shows that you don't have strep throat."

"I get most of my culture from yogurt," I said.

The doctor looked like he was about to get sick. "I am not going to prescribe antibiotics," he said. "Just take some over-the-counter cold medicine and you should be fine."

The day after Sue and I met the twins, I developed a dry cough, probably because it wasn't raining. (Now you know why I never went to med school.)

The symptoms persisted after we got home, where I also started to sneeze. Sue, who didn't want to catch anything, told me not to come near her.

"Do you want me to go to a room with achoo?" I asked.

Sue rolled her eyes, which were heavy, indicating that she was getting sick, too.

She recovered quickly, which is more than I could say for myself, so I went back to the clinic, where another physician asked if I had allergies.

"I'm only allergic to myself," I answered.

"As you get older," she said, sizing me up as older, "you can develop allergies."

She prescribed a nasal spray.

"With the size of my nose, will I need a hose?" I asked, noting that my question rhymed.

"No," the doctor said. "You won't have to call the fire department."

On a return visit to see the twins, I found that Quinn was sick. So was big brother Xavier.

Zoe was starting to come down with something, too.

When I got home, I learned that Chloe and Lilly also were sick.

All the kids got well, but my postnasal drip, or pre-nasal drip, or neo-nasal drip, or whatever the hell I had, was hanging on. I returned to the clinic, where I should have my own parking space, and was given a different spray.

"If this one doesn't work," said a third doctor, "take some antibiotics."

My illness persisted. Finally, after I had run out of medicine, I opened a bottle of blackberry brandy and had a shot.

The following day, I was cured.

"The next time I get sick," I told Sue, "I'm going to take this stuff first."

"My Four Decades of Lip Shtick"

As a man who has sported a mustache for forty years, following in the grand tradition of such hirsute heroes as Mark Twain, Groucho Marx, and my late grandmother, it gives me great pleasure and a persistent itching sensation to announce that I was named Mustached American of the Day.

This honor was bestowed upon me by the American Mustache Institute, an esteemed organization that not only is dedicated to fighting discrimination against people with facial hair, but does not, technically, exist anymore.

"Congratulations on the fortieth anniversary of your mustache!" AMI president Adam Causgrove said when I called to thank him for lowering the otherwise high standards of the institute, which has ceased formal operations but "will live forever in our hearts and on the internet."

AMI, which Causgrove said is headquartered "in my bedroom" in Pittsburgh, plans to resurrect the International Mustache Hall of Fame, whose members include Theodore Roosevelt, Salvador Dali, and Burt Reynolds.

"You could be eligible," he told me, adding: "You don't have to be dead to get in."

But AMI no longer bestows the Robert Goulet Memorial Mustached American of the Year Award, which Causgrove won in 2012 and I came close to winning in 2010.

"That was an impressive showing," said Causgrove, referring to my second-place finish, in which I received eighty-five thousand votes, presumably from people who now suffer from RSI (Repetitive 'Stache Injury).

I lost by a whisker to a Florida firefighter named Brian Sheets but beat out such alleged celebrities as then-major league pitcher Carl Pavano, Washington Post columnist Gene Weingarten, and entertainer Brandon Wardell, who was endorsed by model and actress Brooke Shields.

I was endorsed by Sue, who is the reason I have a mustache.

In 1979, a year after we were married, I had surgery for a deviated septum and afterward was swathed in bandages that covered my tender nose and naked upper lip. I bore a frightening resemblance to Boris Karloff in "The Mummy," mainly because I was not yet "The Daddy."

When the bandages came off, I had a chevron mustache, which does not, unfortunately, get me a discount at Chevron gas stations.

"I like it!" Sue exclaimed, politely not mentioning the rest of my face.

So I kept the lip rug, which I have been told by people with astigmatism makes me look like Tom Selleck, minus the talent, charisma, and money.

"What a heartwarming story!" said Causgrove, who works in corporate relations at Carnegie Mellon University and who for the past eight years has sported his award-winning handlebar mustache, which has the endorsement of his wife, Chelsea, whom he lovingly calls "the first lady of mustachery."

In recognition of my four decades of mustachery, Causgrove issued a proclamation that read, in part:

> *Jerry Zezima Ruby Anniversary of Acclaimed Mouthbrow*
>
> *WHEREAS, In the year 1979, a young Jerry Zezima embarked on a brave and noble journey into the sexually dynamic Mustached American lifestyle.*
>
> *WHEREAS, By embracing his facial foliage ... Jerry has risen to the peaks of his profession in the Stamford, Connecticut-based humor columnist community ...*
>
> *NOW, THEREFORE, I, Chief Executive of the American Mustache Institute, Dr. Adam Paul Causgrove, declare that through a rigorous review process, steeped in the science of nuclear mustacheology and augmented with fine American bourbon ... the Honorable Mr. Jerry Zezima ... is to be saluted, ogled, venerated, and praised — in that particular order."*

"Thank you from the bottom of my mustache," I told Causgrove. "For once in my life, I'm speechless."

"I'm sure your wife would endorse that, too," he said. "And she would agree that it's not just lip service."

"Out to Lunch at Victoria's Secret"

As a thoroughly modern man with a partially feminine side, which I always sit on when I eat lunch, I am not embarrassed to say that if it weren't for Victoria's Secret, I would have gone hungry every day.

That's because Sue, a thoroughly modern woman with no masculine side, and a longtime customer of the clothing and beauty chain, used to pack my lunch in a Victoria's Secret bag.

Before I retired, my second meal of the day was the hit of the office, where colleagues routinely asked what I had for lunch, to which I replied, "I can't tell you. It's a Secret."

When my pink striped bag started to sag under the weight of the incredible edibles packed within, it was time to go to Victoria's Secret to buy Sue a little something. Then I could get a new bag and avoid not only starving each weekday but depriving my office mates of the pleasure of asking if my ham sandwich was wrapped in something frilly.

"May I help you?" sales associate Elana Litsakis asked as Sue and I perused the merchandise.

"I'm looking for a lunch bag," I replied.

Elana, twenty-nine, who said she has "heard it all" from shoppers of the male persuasion, added that this was the first time a guy was more interested in lunch than lingerie.

"I appreciate intimate apparel," I explained. "But the way to a man's heart is through his stomach. And I need something to carry my lunch in."

"Does that mean you're looking for something to wear?" Elana asked Sue, who nodded and replied, "I'd like to see some leggings."

"How about armings?" I wondered.

"They haven't come in yet," said Elana, who showed Sue the selection and directed her to the fitting room while I stood next to the thongs, which Elana was marking, pricing, and, somehow, folding.

"I don't suppose you have anything in my size," I said.

"Of course we do," Elana responded with a smile. "What color would you like?"

"Pink," I said. "It'll match my new bag."

"My grandpa likes our bags," Elana told me. "For his eightieth birthday, we got him a camera that we put in one of them. He said, 'Is there a girl in there, too?'"

"You don't seem to have anything for guys," I said.

"We have cologne," Elana countered. "There's Very Sexy for Him and Very Sexy for Him Platinum."

"What's the difference?" I asked.

"One is Platinum," Elana said. "The other isn't."

"I think I'll stick with Eau de Budweiser," I told her.

When Sue emerged from the fitting room, she said she didn't want the leggings but would buy two sweatshirts instead.

"You get a free panty," Elana said.

"Wow," said Sue.

I agreed.

We thanked Elana for her help and, in my case, her unlimited patience and headed to the checkout, where I told Alexis, the cashier, about my lunchtime cravings.

"You must be very popular," she said as she rang up Sue's purchase. "It comes to seventy dollars," Alexis added. "If you want a bag, it will be an extra five cents."

"I'll buy you two bags," Sue said sweetly, signing a bill for $70.10.

"You spare no expense for me," I said gratefully. "By the way, what's for lunch tomorrow?"

"After this," Sue said, "you can make it yourself."

"Date Night at the Diner"

When it comes to life in the fast lane, Sue and I are on the side of the road with a flat tire. That's why we can't make it to the airport to fly to some exotic locale like the Greek islands.

But on a Saturday night, we did the next best thing and drove to the hottest spot in a city that never wakes: the diner.

This one is owned by a very nice guy named Gus, who was born in Greece.

"Tell me when you want to go and I'll tell you where to go," Gus said.

"People are always telling me where to go," I responded.

"I mean," Gus clarified, "I'll suggest the best places to visit when you and your wife go to Greece."

"Greece is the word," I said, doing him and everyone else in the place a big favor by not singing for my supper.

Instead, Sue and I ordered it from a menu with enough delicious selections to turn me into Zezima the Greek, even though I'm Italian and, according to a DNA test, Martian.

"Would you like anything to drink?" our waiter, Michael, asked pleasantly.

"I'll have a Corona," Sue replied.

"There's no smoking in here," I told her.

"Not a cigar," Sue said with a sigh. "A beer."

Michael dutifully wrote it down, then asked me, "And you, sir?"

"I'll have a Blue Moon," I said.

When Michael returned with our brews, I said, "We don't go out too often. In fact," I added, holding up my bottle, "it's only once in a ..."

"Blue moon!" Michael exclaimed with a laugh. "I got it!"

"Please," Sue said. "Don't encourage him."

I couldn't be discouraged from ordering a jumbo burger with bacon, fries, onion rings, lettuce, tomato, cole slaw, and, the *piece de resistance* (I speak fluent Greek), a pickle.

"I'm really in a pickle now," I told Michael, who laughed again (I think he wanted a generous tip, which he deserved) and took Sue's order, which was the same as mine, minus the bacon.

"Date night at the diner," she said with a smile after the burgers arrived. "Isn't it romantic?"

"Umph, umph, umph," I replied with a mouthful of food.

The burgers were cooked to perfection by Carlo, whom I later visited in the kitchen.

"My wife doesn't like the way I cook burgers because they end up like hockey pucks," I said.

"I don't play hockey," said Carlo, who added that his wife likes the way he cooks everything.

"Customers like it, too," said a waitress named Margaret. "I've worked in places where I didn't eat. The food here is fresh and delicious."

That was evident by the gluttony of the family sitting next to us. Some of them ordered porterhouse steaks the size of anvils.

"That's my favorite item on the menu," Gus told me. "I could eat one every day."

"So could I," I said, "but I want to keep my boyish figure."

When Sue and I were done, Michael, who is Gus's nephew, returned and asked Sue if she wanted a doggy bag for the half-burger she couldn't finish.

"Yes, please," she said.

I had only a leaf of iceberg lettuce left.

"I don't think I'll take it home," I said. "It could be dangerous."

"Why?" asked Michael.

"Because," I explained, "an iceberg sank the Titanic."

He laughed again, earning a ten-dollar tip for a meal that came to thirty-two dollars.

"You spare no expense for me, dear," Sue said sweetly after I also paid for a baklava for her to take home.

"Let me know when you want to go to Greece," Gus said.

"I will," I replied. "And the next time we go out on a hot date, we're coming back to the diner."

CHAPTER 6

(Time for a break so you can get a lesson in Retirement 101. Here are questions and answers, a glossary, a list of famous retirees, and some retirement quotes. And don't worry: There won't be a quiz.)

"Retirement Q&A"

Q. I have just retired and am loving it except for one thing: Every day my wife leaves me a to-do list of things I don't want to do. What should I do?

A. The first thing you should do is throw away the list. The second thing you should do is what you always dreamed of doing in retirement: nothing.

Q. My wife won't like that. Any other suggestions?

A. Do all the things on the to-do list, but do them so badly that your wife will never leave you another to-do list.

Q. My husband has just retired and keeps getting in my way. It's really annoying. Do you have any advice?

A. Send him to the store to buy groceries, but turn off your cellphone so he can't call you every three minutes to ask where things are.

Q. Now that I am not working anymore, my daughter keeps asking me to babysit her kids. I love my grandchildren and always have fun with them, but my daughter says I spoil them. What's your recommendation?

A. Tell your daughter that if you really wanted to spoil your grandchildren, you'd bring them beer and cigars. She'll soon begin to appreciate you and will never complain again. Then, the next time you have to babysit, bring the kids a big bag of candy.

Q. My wife and I are both retired, but we have discovered, after all these years together, that we have very little in common. How can we rekindle our relationship?

A. Try to remember the things that attracted you to each other in the first place. For example, take her out for a romantic dinner. But don't, under any circumstances, ask if she wants the early bird special.

Q. I noticed that a previous questioner said her husband keeps getting in her way. That was my wife. You suggested that she send me shopping, but I can't go every day. What should I do?

A. Get a part-time job. Take up snorkeling. Do anything to get out of the house because if your wife is the beneficiary in your life insurance policy, she will smother you in your sleep. Or, and I realize this is a pretty extreme measure, you could simply stay out of her way.

Q. I am retired and just signed up for unemployment. According to the rules, I have to apply for a job on three separate days every week so I can keep getting benefits, but I don't want to work. What should I do?

A. Apply for jobs you have absolutely no hope of getting. For example, if you were a journalist, look for an opening at a hospital for a brain surgeon, or at a laboratory for a nuclear physicist, or in the National Football League for a middle linebacker. You'll receive an email saying, "Thanks for applying," which you can show to the unemployment office.

Q. What if I actually am offered a job?

A. Don't turn it down! Instead, do one of three things: (a) demand a million dollars a year, plus a company car, preferably a Lamborghini, in which case you won't be hired, (b) accept the job and screw up so royally that you'll be fired, then you can reapply for unemployment, or (c) leave the country until this thing blows over.

Q. When I turned sixty-five, I enrolled in Medicare Part A. Now that I'm retired, I have to get supplemental health insurance through Medicare Part B. It's even been suggested that I sign up for Parts C and D if I want dental and vision coverage. I've called several health-care companies to get rates, but it's all so confusing. The whole process is driving me crazy. Any suggestions?

A. Sign up for Medicare Part Z, which covers insanity.

Q. To avoid going through the entire alphabet, what should I do?

A. Don't get sick.

Q. Now that I'm retired, I have time to do the things I didn't have time to do before, like go back to school, or take acting lessons, or possibly write a book, though not like this one because even I couldn't write a book this bad. Still, I'd love to follow my dreams, but I'm afraid it's too late. What's your advice?

A. It's only too late when you're dead, so get off your duff and make those dreams come true. Good luck. And have fun!

"Retirement Glossary"

Alarm clock: A device for waking you out of a sound sleep at an ungodly hour so you can sit in rush-hour traffic on the way to a job you hate. Once you're retired, you will never need one again.

Free time: The rest of your life.

The rest of your life: An indefinite period in which you don't have as much free time as you had hoped.

Babysitting: Either what you do for your grandchildren or what your spouse does for you.

Pajamas: Daytime attire when you don't have to go anyplace.

Happy hour: Formerly the period directly after work, it's now any time of day that can be described as "it's five o'clock somewhere."

Coffee: A liquid that used to keep you awake during the day but which now keeps you awake at night.

Nap: A brief stretch of sleep that gives you the energy to relax for the rest of the day.

Exercise: A form of physical fitness that used to involve going to the gym but which now includes such activities as lifting your grandchildren, searching the house for your glasses, and getting up twice a night to go to the bathroom.

Intimacy: Snuggling up to your spouse so you can watch home improvement shows.

"Famous Retirees"

George Washington: The first president of the United States, he initially retired from army life before serving two terms as chief executive. He could have stayed in office indefinitely but decided he'd had enough, ensuring a peaceful transfer of power that set the tone for our democracy. Unfortunately, Washington spent much of his retirement with dental problems that weren't covered under his medical plan.

Brett Favre: NFL quarterback who, like many other sports stars (including **Deion Sanders**, **Rob Gronkowski**, **Michael Jordan**, **Magic Johnson**, **Yogi Berra**, **Dizzy Dean**, and **Satchel Paige**), retired but later came back because, presumably, they missed the action, the money, and not having to do chores around the house.

Curly Howard: The most popular member of the Three Stooges comedy team had to retire in his forties because of health problems. Do modern-day retirees still revere him? Soitenly! Nyuk, nyuk, nyuk!

Curly Neal: Basketball legend who starred with the Harlem Globetrotters. The team retired his number (22) after he retired — and, to his credit, didn't come back. He got his nickname because his shaved head resembled that of Curly Howard (see above).

James Michael Curley: Colorfully corrupt politician who served as mayor of Boston and governor of Massachusetts. His single term as governor was described by a biographer as "a disaster mitigated only by moments of farce." Sounds like he was even more incompetent than Curly Howard (see two above). He also served in the state House of Representatives and retired only after voters stopped electing him to public office.

"Retirement Quotes"

"The trouble with retirement is that you never get a day off." — *Abe Lemons, college basketball player and coach*

"Retirement is like a long vacation in Las Vegas. The goal is to enjoy it to the fullest, but not so fully that you run out of money." — *Jonathan Clements, author and scriptwriter*

"A retired husband is often a wife's full-time job." — *Ella Harris, author*

"Retirement's the most wonderful thing. I get to enjoy all the things I never stopped to notice on the way up. After an extraordinary life, it's time to enjoy my retirement." — *Patrick Macnee, actor*

"I found out retirement means playing golf, or I don't know what the hell it means. But to me, retirement means doing what you have fun doing." — *Dick Van Dyke, comedian and entertainer*

"We work all our lives so we can retire — so we can do what we want with our time — and the way we define or spend our time defines who we are and what we value." — *Bruce Linton, author*

"As your life changes, it takes time to recalibrate, to find your values again. You might also find that retirement is the time when you stretch out and find your potential." — *Sid Miramontes, author*

"Retirement: That's when you return from work one day and say, 'Hi, Honey, I'm home — forever.'" — *Gene Perret, comedy writer*

"Don't act your age in retirement. Act like the inner young person you have always been." — *John Anthony West, author*

CHAPTER 7

(What, you didn't think there were more grandparenting adventures? They never end. And I don't want them to.)

"How to Bathe a Baby"

Even though I haven't taken a bath since I was a baby, which dates all the way back to the administration of Dwight D. Eisenhower, whose bathing habits are classified information, I am now an expert on the subject. That's because I gave a bath to a baby who needed it so badly, after her diaper exploded all over me, that I would have taken one, too, except I couldn't fit in the sink.

All of this happened at three a.m., a time when babies (and their grandfathers) should be sleeping like babies. I would have been except that Zoe and Quinn woke up hungry, which meant they had to be changed, then fed, then changed again, and again, and again.

In the end, which is where the worst of it came out, a bath was in order.

Before you get to that point, however, you will notice that babies are trained to follow a very strict routine that requires them to go through several diapers, onesies, burp cloths, towels, baby wipes, table pads, bassinet covers, and, if they haven't already been kicked off, socks.

The number one concern is, of course, number one, which can soak a diaper so thoroughly that it weighs more than the baby.

This is followed by the number two concern, which is followed by number three (a combination of the first two) and number four (a regurgitation of the entire contents of the bottle, which can burst like lava from the front end of the child and land all over your shirt, pants, and, if they haven't already been kicked off, socks).

If you are in charge of twins, as I was, you have eight concerns. But on this particular night, Zoe outdid her little (by two pounds) brother by emitting two pounds of the aforementioned substances.

Lacking a power washer, which is great for getting baby effluent off the side of the house, I decided to give Zoe a bath.

The first thing I had to do was take off all her clothes. Or I would have if I could fit into them. I'm glad I couldn't because they didn't need to be laundered so much as incinerated, but I didn't want to call the fire department in the middle of the night because: (a) it would have awakened Quinn, who had finally gone back to sleep, and (b) my own clothes were almost as filthy as Zoe's and would have repulsed even the bravest smoke eater.

I filled the sink with warm water that covered most of the baby tub, which features a mesh seat on which I placed Zoe, who looked up at me with teary eyes as if to say, "Here's another fine mesh you've gotten me into."

Then she started to squirm. Wet babies and greased pigs are extremely difficult to grasp, although why anybody would want to grease a pig — or change its diaper — is even harder to grasp.

I took a small washcloth, wet it, and squirted on some baby wash, which was "pediatrician recommended" and "lightly scented." Even a pediatrician knows that a light scent can't mask a heavy one, so I used more soap and worked Zoe into a lather. Her continued squirming worked me into one.

I scrubbed and rinsed her, shampooed her hair, and engaged her in baby talk, which I was glad nobody else could hear because Zoe didn't sound nearly as infantile as I did.

Afterward, I dried her off, dressed her, and put her in her bassinet, where she fell fast asleep.

Then it was my turn to come clean. I took off all my clothes and got in the shower. I would have taken a bath, but I ran out of baby wash.

"Too Cuticle for Words"

Sometimes, a boy just likes to feel pretty. In my case, that would involve plastic surgery.

You can count on the fingers of one hand the number of times I have put the "man" in manicure. And I have put my worst foot forward even less frequently to get a pedicure.

But I discovered that I like to make others feel pretty, which is why I opened Poppie's Beauty Salon and Nail Spa. The first customers were Chloe and Lilly.

The girls are into fashion and love to get the spa treatment. I have a fashion plate in my head, which means I am more likely to go to a saloon than a salon.

Still, when they asked me to paint their toenails, I resolved to be a beaut of a beautician and make their piggies as pretty as a picture.

The first thing I needed, of course, was nail polish. Since Sue wasn't home, I went through her drawers and stole a few bottles.

"I want pink, Poppie!" said Chloe, who sported rainbow fingernails painted a couple of days earlier by Lauren.

"Me, too!" agreed Lilly, whose fingernails were bright red.

Initially the girls couldn't decide between red and purple for their tootsies but settled on pink because it matched their unicorn pajamas.

Since it was the morning after a sleepover, I also wore pajamas. They were blue with egg and sausage stains from breakfast, which is part of the service at Poppie's Beauty Salon and Nail Spa.

In addition to polish, my equipment consisted of a nail file, which I used to file the girls' nails (file this under "duh"); a hair dryer, which I used on the wet polish (it was easier than a ceiling fan); and paper towels, strips of which I stuck between the girls' toes so the polish wouldn't get smudged (when you can't find cotton balls, you have to improvise).

But first, I gave each of the girls a foot massage.

"That tickles, Poppie!" shrieked Chloe, breaking out in giggles.

Then I started to apply the polish.

"Hold perfectly still," I instructed as Chloe sat in a chair and I carefully painted the big toenail on her right foot.

Some of the polish got on the toe itself, but I immediately wiped it off.

"Poppie needs more coffee," I said as I continued down the other four toenails, after which I started on her left foot.

The hardest part was not applying either too much or too little polish. By the time I got to Chloe's last toe, I had it all figured out.

Next it was Lilly's turn. I grabbed her right foot and, pinching each toe, chirped: "This little piggy went to market, this little piggy stayed home, this little piggy had roast beef, this little piggy had none. And this little piggy went wee, wee, wee all the way home."

"I don't have to go wee-wee," said Lilly, who was eager to get it over with.

It didn't help that she sneezed a couple of times as I applied polish that had to be wiped off her pinky toes.

When the pedicures were done, the girls sat in the family room, their toenails pretty in pink.

"Nice job, Poppie!" Chloe exclaimed.

"Yeah!" Lilly chimed in.

"Should I paint my toenails, too?" I asked.

"No!" the girls responded in unison.

"Don't you want me to look pretty?" I said.

"Boys don't look pretty," Chloe declared. "They look handsome."

"You're handsome, Poppie," said Lilly.

Chloe agreed.

"Thank you, girls," I said. "You just saved me a fortune in plastic surgery."

"Naps Are Not Fake Snooze"

If there is one thing I have learned in my new career as a babysitter, aside from the lamentable fact that my grandchildren are more mature than I am, it's that napping is very important to both kids and geezers.

I found this out during a weeklong stay in which I babysat Zoe and Quinn and beat them at their own game by sleeping on the job.

Of course, I didn't sleep while they were awake, or even while one of them was awake and the other asleep, but I did doze off while both of them napped, which refreshed me so much that it was practically a full hour after they both woke up before I needed another nap.

The problem with naps is that infants need them but don't always want them and oldsters either want them but don't always have time or don't want them but slowly come to the realization that they need them because they are, after all, old.

According to Katie, Zoe is "a good napper" and Quinn is "a bad napper."

They both seemed pretty good to me, even when they weren't on the same napping schedule, because one or both of them would nap anywhere from twenty minutes to three hours.

This gave me time, when their naps coincided, to catch a few Z's myself.

And I needed the rest because most of the time, one would be up and the other down, or one would want to eat and the other wouldn't, or I'd start to feed one and then, five minutes later, the other would want to eat, too, or one would need to be changed and the other would fuss until I had the first one cleaned up, then I'd have to change the other one's diaper as well.

No wonder I was fatigued.

Unfortunately, I couldn't always get to sleep while both kids were napping because I was too wired to be tired. I solved the dilemma by watching daytime TV, which had such a soporific effect that I was soon snoozing contentedly and dreaming about bottles and diapers.

My reverie was often interrupted by crying. This was a signal that one of the twins was awake and needed to be fed, changed, or both. Sometimes, however, I merely dreamed that one of them was awake. So I went back to sleep. Two minutes later, one of them was awake for real and my nap was cut short.

Then I had to put the kids in clean outfits. These diabolical articles of baby clothing feature either snaps or zippers. The ones with snaps were obviously designed by sadists whose job is to stymie exhausted grandfathers who can't line up the snaps properly. Needless to say, but I will say it anyway, they are not a snap.

The ones with zippers are easier but still troublesome when the baby kicks so furiously that the aforementioned grandfathers get their fingers caught or otherwise can't get the outfit fastened. This often prompted me to say to either Zoe or Quinn, "Go out there and win one for the zipper."

They had no idea what I was saying, but it made me feel better.

It also made me tired again. But I couldn't take another nap until both children were taking one, too.

Still, naps are not a sign of old age. They are a pleasantly restorative experience that puts you in touch with your younger self and gives you the energy necessary to be a good babysitter.

Now that I'm retired, I like to nap even when I'm not watching the kids. As most geezers would agree, it works like a dream.

"Baking Lesson Really Pans Out"

I never thought baking was a piece of cake, mainly because I'm half-baked. But I learned that I could have my cake and eat it, too, after getting a baking lesson from my grandson.

Xavier is hot stuff when it comes to the culinary arts. I, on the other hand, which should have sported a pot-holder, have always believed that if you can't stand the heat, get out of the kitchen.

Contrary to this brilliant advice, which has prevented me from burning the house down, I got into the kitchen to watch Xavier help Dave prepare a fish dinner. He also helped make pizza. But the *pièce de résistance*, a French phrase meaning "resist a piece of anything I have made," was the cake Xavier baked with Sue, without whom I would have starved to death long ago.

While Xavier never got close to a hot stove and didn't have access to sharp implements, he did climb up on his step stool to help wash or mix ingredients for various dishes and pour them into pots, pans, and bowls in the preparation of everything from entrees to desserts.

"If I'm in the kitchen, Xavier has to be there, too," said Dave, adding that his father, Bob, is a great guy but not exactly a culinary artist.

My late father, the original Jerry Zezima, was also a great guy and made the world's best salad, but he couldn't match the cooking skills of my mother, Rosina, a kitchen magician who should have her own Food Network show, or my sisters, Susan (who recently showed me how to make chicken that could wow anyone except, of course, a chicken) and Elizabeth (who once had to show me how to make a grilled cheese sandwich).

My one culinary triumph came about twenty years ago, when I was first runner-up in the pasta sauce division of the Newman's Own and Good Housekeeping Recipe Contest for a dish I called Zezima's Zesty Ziti Zinger. Paul Newman himself polished off a bowl of the stuff and raved about it. That the legendary actor is, at the present time, deceased is purely coincidental.

Because my next-best creation is microwave popcorn, I was in awe of Xavier's budding talent.

Among his toys is the Melissa & Doug Prepare & Serve Pasta Set, which I should borrow for another batch of ziti. But his favorite is the Melissa & Doug Baking Play Set, which includes a baking tin, measuring cups, a whisk, a spatula, a rolling pin, and an oven mitt, which he wore when he and Sue baked a cake.

The ingredients were Betty Crocker Super Moist Rainbow Chip Cake Mix and Pillsbury Confetti Funfetti Vanilla Flavored Frosting.

As I watched, Xavier handed Sue two eggs, which he wouldn't break.

"If you did," I told him, "the yolk would be on you."

"Can't you find something else to do?" Sue asked.

"Not at the moment," I answered as Xavier stood on his step stool next to a bowl on the counter and poured milk over the eggs and cake mix. Then he used a spatula to create a creamy batter.

"Batter up!" I exclaimed.

Xavier smiled. Sue didn't.

They both poured the mixture into a pan, which Sue placed in the oven. When the cake was done, Xavier spread on the frosting, which he topped with rainbow sprinkles.

The cake was a masterpiece. And it tasted even better than it looked.

"This is delicious, Xavier!" I said, licking sprinkles out of my mustache.

The little boy beamed.

"I hope you learned something," Sue said to me.

"I did," I replied. "Getting a baking lesson from our grandson was the icing on the cake."

"Little Shoppers Give Me Food for Thought"

Whenever I go to the grocery store, I am the designated driver for Sue, who likes to say, after I get lost in the beer aisle, that I put the cart before the horse's aft.

So I was grateful to get a food shopping demonstration from Chloe and Lilly, each of whom was a "customer in training."

That's what it said on the sign above their little carts, which are designed to let youngsters shop with their parents and grandparents and stock up on ice cream, cookies, and other goodies that they would consume exclusively if only their parents and grandparents would let them.

In addition to Chloe and Lilly, the supermarket expedition featured me, Sue, and Lauren. Everyone had a cart except yours truly because, I am sure, they were afraid I would stock up on beer, munchies, and other goodies that I would consume exclusively if only my wife would let me.

One thing I noticed about the kiddie carts was that they each had four wheels that all went in the same direction. This is never the case with regular carts, which have wheels that go north, south, east, and west all at the same time.

If cars were like that, you'd have a fender bender every day and your insurance rates would go up so much that the only mode of transportation you could afford would be, of course, a shopping cart.

As we navigated the store, an older gentleman came around the corner with his cart and said to Chloe, "If I had known you were going to be here, I'd ask you to do my shopping, too."

Chloe, whose cart was already half-full with items that included cereal and oranges, which Lauren put in there instead of ice cream and cookies, smiled and replied, "I'm shopping with Mommy."

I said to the guy, "She's a customer in training."

"She could teach me a thing or two," he said, adding: "Where's your cart?"

"I'm a bad driver," I explained. "Training wouldn't help."

Lilly, meanwhile, started to load up her cart with sweets.

"She's trying to sneak them in," Lauren told me. Then she said to Lilly, "Put them back."

Lilly grumbled and handed them to me so I could restock the shelf.

A nice lady passed me in the aisle and said, "You're doing a good job. Maybe you could work here."

"It would get me out of the house," I said. "But I'd get fired for eating the profits."

The store was filled with so many customers and their carts that it looked like rush hour in a construction zone. I was afraid tempers would flare so much that there would be a drive-by shouting.

But everyone was very nice and accommodating for the girls, who routinely cut off other shoppers in an effort to keep up with Lauren and Sue. I tried to play traffic cop, though even if I had a whistle, it wouldn't have done any good.

Finally, we got to the checkout area, where the girls brought their carts so the contents could be rung up.

"You're a good shopper," a cashier named Ann told Chloe.

"Thank you," Chloe said as she handed Ann several items for scanning.

"Are you going to pay for them?" Ann asked.

"No," said Chloe. "Mommy is."

Lilly went with Sue to another cashier, a young man named Eric, who said she did a good job.

"I know," Lilly told him.

On the way out, Sue said to me, "The girls are better food shoppers than you are."

"You're right," I admitted. "They even made sure I didn't get lost in the beer aisle."

CHAPTER 8

(Where did I get my inspiration as a retiree? Why isn't retirement a good fit for some people? And how do friends and former colleagues feel about it? Here, as an old newspaperman would say, is the scoop.)

"All in the Family"

Even when I was working, I knew that my mom, Rosina Zezima, was the mother of all retirees.

At ninety-five, she is sharper than I am. It's a dubious achievement, of course, because bathroom sponges also fall into this category, but there is no denying that my mother is amazing.

So was my father, the original and best Jerry Zezima, a man of deep love and quiet humor who was married to my mother for sixty-two years before he died in 2011 at age ninety-three.

We miss him still. But he was brought back, in vivid memory, when I talked with my mother about their life in retirement.

"I wanted to give him cooking lessons," recalled my mother, who was still working as a registered nurse when my father retired from his forty-year career at Perkin-Elmer Corp. in Norwalk, Connecticut, where he was a supervisor. "He said no way. The best he could do was make toast, tea, or coffee. He could make an egg once in a while and he could heat up leftovers."

"He did make a mean dish of macaroni with oil and garlic," I said.

"Yes, he did," my mother acknowledged. "And he was a great salad maker."

My father also was the handiest guy I ever knew. He came up with all kinds of little inventions, like a light bulb changer that featured a funnel at the end of a stick. He loved to putter around the house.

"And he was the best window washer you could ever find," said my mother, adding that he also liked to work outside.

"I can picture him out in the yard, digging a hole where he found a big rock," my mother said. "He would get an iron pole and put it underneath the rock and, with all his might, little by little, waltz that rock right out of the hole. He also built a few walls. He made an apron around the yard. He was lost in the kitchen, as you know, so it was the only kind of apron he used."

My father loved retirement and always found something to do. His favorite thing was watching his grandchildren: Katie and Lauren as well as my sister Susan's children, Taylor, Blair, and Whitney.

"He took me fishing," Lauren remembered. "I loved it. When I caught a fish, he was even more excited than I was."

Four years after my father retired, my mother did, too.

"We traveled, we went dancing, we did things together," my mother said. "We finally had time for each other, even if it was just going shopping or watching TV, and it was wonderful."

My father had a physical decline that lasted about two years, during which my mother cared for him with love and devotion. When he passed, she was sad, naturally, but she also was determined to live her life to the fullest.

Still, there were some bumps. Four, to be exact, caused by falls.

The first fall, when my mother was eighty-nine, broke the femur in her left leg. A hospital stay and a long rehab followed. My mother's goal was to heal well enough to travel from Stamford to Long Island for Chloe's baptism. She made it, in a wheelchair, with her spirits and good cheer intact.

The next tumble, two years later, broke her wrist. Like the first time, she bounced back.

At ninety-three, she fell and broke three vertebrae in her back. Ditto.

At ninety-four, my mother fell and hit her head, which, she said, is "too hard to break." After yet another round of rehab, she was as good as (almost) new.

On her ninety-fifth birthday, we had a party at her house, where she still lives. My sister Susan, a three-time cancer survivor with a huge heart and a fabulous sense of humor, lives with her and is her primary caregiver. Blair lives there, too, and is fantastically helpful.

My sister Elizabeth, who lives about half an hour away, is at the house regularly and handles my mother's finances. She is a commodities cargo operations manager who lost her job when she was sixty-three but quickly got another one. She is active politically, also has a sharp wit, and doesn't plan to retire just yet.

Now that I am retired, I get to see my sisters more often. It's great. We have a close, loving bond and we laugh a lot.

I see my mother, too, of course. And we talk every day. It's a pleasure. She's unfailingly positive and cheerful. She gets around with her trusty rollator, keeps up on the news, loves seeing or talking with her grandchildren, and adores her great-grandchildren, who know her as Gigi.

"Life is still good," said my mother, who has a coffee mug with the words: "Retired, Not Expired." And, she added, "I intend to keep it that way."

"The Good, the Bad, and the Iffy"

Retirement isn't for everybody. My father-in-law, Carmine Pikero, was an example.

"He retired at sixty-one from the phone company and he was very unhappy," recalled my mother-in-law, Jo Pikero. "I was still working and he didn't have anything to do, so he got his real estate license. He sold a couple of properties."

It wasn't very fulfilling, said my mother-in-law, who was an executive assistant at a real estate company in Stamford. When she retired, six years after my father-in-law did, things were different.

"We traveled a lot," said my mother-in-law, adding that they loved to go on cruises.

Like my father, my father-in-law wasn't exactly a master chef.

"The only thing he did was grill, like you do, Jerry," my mother-in-law told me. "And at Christmas, he would stuff the calamari. Do you do that?"

"No," I confessed.

"Now that you have time, you should learn," she said.

My father-in-law died in 2015 and my mother-in-law misses him very much.

"It's not the same," she said. "Retirement can be lonely without your spouse."

Some people get other jobs after they retire. Sue and I met one of them when we went to a home improvement store.

"I got in my wife's hair," said Bob, sixty-five. "I had to get out of the house, so I got a job here."

I met Joe, sixty-three, a road crew supervisor, when he was overseeing the milling and paving of my street.

"I retired from the Army, then I got this job," he told me.

"Why didn't you stay retired?" I asked.

Joe smiled and said, "I have three kids and I get them whatever they want."

I met Toni on a flight that was supposed to go from New York to Washington but had to turn back because of a mechanical problem.

"I've been retired for fifteen years," said Toni, who worked for twenty-two years as vice president of corporate affairs for Time-Warner. Now she's an innkeeper.

"I love it," she said. "I meet all kinds of people."

"What kind of person am I?" I asked.

"A very nice one," Toni replied. "And you look too young to be retired."

"So do you," I said.

Toni smiled and said, "It helps to be young at heart."

"I'm young at head," I said. "That helps, too."

On another flight, there was Arch, seventy-two, whom Sue and I met when we were coming back from seeing Katie and her family in Washington.

"I retired, I got bored, so I applied for a job as a flight attendant," he told us when he came by with the beverage and snack cart. "I get good benefits and frequent flyer miles. What can I get you?"

"I'll have a ginger ale and a bag of almonds," I said.

"And you?" Arch asked Sue.

"Water and Cheez-Its," she said, adding: "You used to get wine."

"I know," said Arch. "But it's a quick flight and you can have a glass when you get home. In fact, you can have as much as you want. And just think: When you retire, you won't have to worry about getting up early the next morning."

"The Best of Friends"

Along with Sue and yours truly, Hank Richert, Tim Lovelette, Peter Keefe, and Clay Hughes were in the notorious Class of 1975 at Saint Michael's College in Colchester, Vermont.

We raised so much hell that we should have sued the makers of "National Lampoon's Animal House," the hilarious 1978 movie starring John Belushi and other assorted ruffians, for theft of intellectual property.

All of us have stayed friends for lo these many years. In fact, we were going to get together for our forty-fifth reunion at St. Mike's, not only to reminisce over refreshing beverages but to take down any "Wanted" posters of us that may still be hanging up. Unfortunately, the eagerly anticipated and potentially riotous homecoming was called off due to the coronavirus pandemic.

So I spoke with Hank, Tim, Peter, and Clay over the phone to get their views on retirement.

Hank Richert

Hank, Sue, and I met in high school, Stamford Catholic, where we were in the not-quite-notorious but certainly memorable Class of 1971.

Hank and I were college roommates for three years and later served as the best man at each other's wedding.

Even though we both majored in political science at Saint Michael's, Hank embarked on a business career and I went into journalism, lacking the skills to be a successful businessman or anything else that would have required me to actually work for a living.

Hank and his wife, Angela, raised two sons, John and Chris, both accomplished young men. John and his wife, Anna, have a toddler daughter, Julia, who is Hank and Angela's only (so far) grandchild.

Hank has traveled extensively during his career, including trips to Europe, Japan, and across the United States. He and Angela have moved around quite a bit, too, living in Georgia, Connecticut, New Jersey, Connecticut again, Virginia, Illinois, and, now, South Carolina, where they will stay when Hank retires.

"I'm counting the weeks," Hank said during our conversation, which was on speakerphone so Angela and Sue could chime in.

Hank has always been driven to do good work and now he is driven to retire. And what better way to do it than by driving a cool set of wheels.

"I got myself a brand-new Ford Mustang GT convertible," Hank said excitedly.

"It's his retirement car," Angela added. "I'm glad he's happy with it. The smile on his face is worth it. He's worked hard all these years."

As of this writing, Hank is still working in business development management, but he plans to call it a career soon.

"You've told me how much you like retirement," Hank said.

"I do," I said. "But I'm driving an SUV."

"You've got to get a Mustang," Angela said. "You should definitely do something to shock your children. We shocked our kids for a change. They didn't think we would do anything so radical and reckless because we've always been practical parents. When the boys heard about the new car, they said, 'Dad bought a Mustang? What!'"

"Actually," said Hank, "Chris had bought one. I drove it a couple of times and said, 'Wow, I like this car. I have to get one of these.' Dealers are hungry because of the pandemic, so we made an appointment. Of course, we had to wear masks. I found three cars that I liked. This one had the most options, so I bought it. I'm really enjoying it."

So are the neighbors.

"We live close to a lake," Hank said. "Come down to visit. We'll rent a boat, fill the cooler with our favorite beverages, and go out on the lake together. Besides, I need an excuse to wear my Speedo."

"No, no, no!" Angela squealed.

"I've had a lot of requests from women in the neighborhood," Hank reported. "They're all asking, 'When are you going to wear your Speedo?'"

Said Angela, "They're looking forward to seeing you drive with the top down."

"I'll put the top down and take you guys out for a drive," Hank told us.

"That would be awesome!" replied Sue, adding: "All I have in my car is a sun roof."

"I have a cloud roof," I said.

Angela, who is two years younger than Hank, can't wait for him to retire.

"He robbed the cradle," said Angela, who was a supervisor at Southern New England Telephone in Connecticut and worked in regulatory services and human resources at Southern Bell in Georgia but left the workforce when John was born.

She did a lot of volunteer work and was on various PTA boards. For fourteen years, she traveled back and forth to Connecticut to help care for her widowed father until his death in 2020.

"Now it's our time," Angela said.

Hank agreed.

"When the pandemic is over, we'd like to go down to Florida to see Julia again," he said. "We do Google Duo with her, John, and Anna, but it's not the same as seeing them in person."

"What else are you looking forward to?" I asked.

"I want to do things I like to do when I want to do them and not be beholden to a schedule," Hank said. "I'm done with getting on planes, being packed in, and staying over in musty hotels."

"We just put a porch on the house," Angela said. "And we got a new grill."

"One of my retirement goals is to be a better barbecue cook," said Hank, adding that he has an even better goal.

"After I retire," he told me, "we should get together and do an Old Farts Podcast."

"With that name, it would get people to listen," Angela said. "When you guys get together, you're very funny."

"It's a million-dollar idea," I said.

"I'd be happy if it's a ten-dollar idea," said Hank.

"Let's do it," I said. "If that doesn't shock the children, nothing will."

Tim Lovelette

Tim was the mastermind behind our most outrageous pranks in college and has been a close friend ever since.

He and Peter Keefe lived in the dorm room next to the one Hank and I lived in during our freshman and sophomore years at St. Mike's.

Tim moved off-campus in our junior year, when he got married. His wife, Jane, whom he met in first grade and began dating in high school, is the backbone of the family, just like Sue and Angela.

"And she still says I'm better than nothing," said Tim, who lives with Jane on Cape Cod, Massachusetts, where they raised three terrific children: Marshall, Amy, and Brendan. Tim and Jane also have six grandchildren.

"I'm sitting here with a glass of Singani 63 brandy and a Chief Cool Arrow cigar, killing the coronavirus from the inside and contemplating retirement," said Tim, who owns Marshall K. Lovelette Insurance, a third-generation agency on the Cape that was founded by Tim's late father.

Tim doesn't have the virus, but he did have prostate cancer.

"The easiest thing I ever did was beating cancer," he said. "What happened after that was worse. Nobody could figure out what was wrong with me. Two weeks after the surgery to remove my prostate, I was in excruciating pain. I couldn't walk for four months. This doctor in the pain clinic, with every degree in the world, he reads my file and says, 'I still can't believe what you've gone through.' I was within hours of dying. I had sepsis, which is bad stuff. I still have infections. Now you'd think, after all that, I would retire. Everyone says, 'Why don't you stop working?' I can't. I'm incapable."

"So you won't ever retire?" I asked.

"Let's just say I'm easing into it," said Tim, who has turned over the day-to-day operation of the business to older son Marshall, who was named after Tim's father. "Besides, retirement itself can kill you."

That's because, according to Tim, women get to retire but men don't.

"Your wife's only concern is to make sure you're not retired," he said. "Men don't retire, they just change bosses. Guys want to be retired, but their wives won't tolerate it. If I retired, Jane would kill me with stuff to do. I have to work to stay alive. I feel sorry for guys like you. You've got three or four more years to live. I can string this thing out forever."

Still, Tim appreciates Jane as much as I appreciate Sue.

"Jane's a saint," he said. "She keeps telling me that. I was in the hospital five times and she stayed with me all the time. I consider your wife to be a saint, too. She's the kindest, nicest person you know, aside from me. But let's face it, Jerry, she's sick to death of you."

"She told me that," I acknowledged. "We've been quarantined together and it's given her a good idea of what life would be like with me if she retired. I think she's having second thoughts. What about Jane?"

"She knows I'm impossible to live with," Tim said of his wife, who has worked in the office at the insurance agency. "Now we're quarantined, too. That means Jane can't babysit the grandkids anymore, although we do have story hour over FaceTime. At this point in time, I'm not retired, so I can remember all their names. If you're retired, they give you the old retiree quiz and ask about your grandkids' dates of birth. If you can't answer, they shake their heads and say, 'He's slipping.'"

"Aside from trying to remember your grandchildren's names and birthdays, what would you do if you did retire?" I asked.

"I don't know," Tim answered. "In the first ten years I worked for my father, there was no vacation allowed. He was strict. He went on vacation, but I couldn't. Then he retired, but he came into the office all the time. He did what I'm doing — pretending to be retired."

At least Tim can keep his business cards, which read:

Tim Lovelette

Musician
Poet
The Epitome of Excellence

He has another one he inherited from a friend on the Cape.

"It said, 'Capt. Moe Johnson: Virgins converted, computers verified, bongo drums, screen doors, nails.' Stuff like that," said Tim, who has always had boats. "I said to Moe, 'When you die, I want your business card.' Well, Moe died and I got both his ashes and the card. Now it says, 'Capt. Tim Lovelette' and all that other stuff."

For many years Tim had a charter boat.

"I was doing professional boating as a sideline," Tim said. "I sold the charter boat and got a smaller boat. I still have a captain's license, but I retired from the charter boat business. That was the one thing I didn't want to retire from."

"Retired or not," I said, "you're still the epitome of excellence."

"Don't tell that to Jane," said Tim. "She'd never believe it."

Peter Keefe

Peter's family moved to the Cape in 1966, and he went to high school with Tim and Jane, so it was natural that he and Tim would be college roommates.

Peter was the right-hand man for a lot of Tim's pranks, like the one they pulled early freshman year. They waited for me and Hank to go to dinner, then took all the furniture out of our room. If that weren't enough, Tim brought up a dog he found in the quad and put the pooch in the empty room.

The dog was released, happy and unharmed, but we never knew what Tim and Peter would be up to, so we adhered to an old saying: If you can't beat 'em, join 'em.

The school has never been the same.

When Tim moved off-campus in junior year, Peter roomed with a fun guy named Denny Smith. Unlike another fun guy, Rick Lajoie, a teetotaler, Denny helped me keep the beer industry afloat.

Peter was a fun guy, too, but he was serious about his studies, earning a degree in English literature.

After graduation, he embarked on a career as a technical writer.

"I was one of the lucky ones," Peter said. "I did what I majored in at Saint Michael's."

He got his first job in May of 1977 in Greenwich, Connecticut.

"Hank was gracious enough to offer his parents' place in Stamford for me to stay," Peter recalled. "I gave myself two weeks to find a job. I had an interview at a technical publishing company in Greenwich the first week. By the end of the second week, I had the job. I was to be a technical writer and editor, and that work became my whole career for the next forty-one years."

This first job entailed working for a trade magazine that covered pollution control equipment. The EPA had just been created and protecting the environment was the hot topic.

"I was immediately given the title of editor," Peter said. "I had a column at the back of the magazine that summarized pollution manufacturers' equipment brochures to entice readers to buy. I produced a monthly newsletter separate from the magazine Then they started sending me on assignments to write feature articles. I went to a Scott Paper Company plant in Maine to write an article on their cutting-edge pollution control measures. I went to many trade shows, the best of which had the show sponsors take over Disneyland in L.A. for a night. Everything at Disneyland was free, and I went on Space Mountain five times. It was a great first-time job. I had an expense account and an American Express card. I had never had a credit card in my life. This was my first dress-up job, and I had to wear a tie every day. I was twenty-four and feeling pretty cool."

Peter was in the magazine job for about two years before the company was sold.

"The new owners wanted to move us to New York City," he said. "I love the city, but I didn't want a daily train commute, so I luckily got a job in the advertising department at ARCO in Greenwich. ARCO was a Fortune 500 company, so it was a step up, and the demands of advertising meant more writing creativity. One of the best events was a sales meeting in Florida, for which I wrote the division president's opening speech to the attendees, complete with a slide show of new products. I ran the slide show in sync with the speech. I was a nervous wreck, but everything went well."

Eventually, Peter moved back to the Cape. He worked at Raytheon in Hyannis and various other high-tech companies around Boston, like RCA and GTE. In the early 1990s, he moved to Virginia and remained a technical writer for the next twenty-six years.

Now Peter lives in Pennsylvania, where he has retired with his partner, Charlie Walker.

"We were wondering where we were going to retire," Peter said. "We were thinking about going farther west in Virginia. One weekend, I was driving to Syracuse for my niece's graduation. My sister's mother-in-law lives in Carlisle, Pennsylvania, and I stayed with her overnight. I immediately loved the town. Some months later, Charlie and I visited Carlisle and thought it might be a good place to retire. Long story short, or short story long, here we are."

Peter retired at age sixty-five. Charlie retired the previous year after working on the international help desk of an airline manufacturer for many years.

"We haven't regretted a minute of it," said Peter, who loves retirement. "The best part for me is not getting up at five o'clock in the morning. I was an early riser for most of my jobs. I liked to go in early because I didn't want to get home at suppertime. But on some mornings, especially in winter, the alarm would go off and I'd think,

'It can't be time to get up.' Also, I don't really miss the whole getting yourself ready for work thing day after day."

The hardest adjustment early on, said Peter, was not having a routine in place.

"Suddenly, after retiring, I'd say, 'What am I going to do today?' Friends already retired had told me that the days will go faster than you think," Peter said. "They are right. There are times when Charlie and I will say, 'My God, the afternoon's gone already.' Pre-virus, we'd go out to lunch almost every day. Being new to Carlisle, we got valuable references to doctors, car mechanics, plumbers, etc., through restaurant contacts. We could eat and get to know a new area all at the same time."

Peter and Charlie have found ways to fill their days.

"I do crosswords," Peter said. "I play cards online. I read like crazy and have to have a book or two going at all times. I walk and exercise five times a week. We watch tons of movies online and from our collection. All in all, retirement's wonderful if you plan ahead. We couldn't be happier."

Clay Hughes

After Hank moved out of the dorm, Clay and I were roommates in our senior year at Saint Michael's.

Clay was the strong, silent type, but with a great sense of fun. He proved it by using that strength to break his own hand.

"We got into a wrestling match in the room," I remembered.

"That's right," Clay said. "I picked you up and slammed you down. My hand hit the metal edge of my bed."

A doctor put Clay in a cast that extended up to the elbow. It covered his broken hand but left most of his digits free. The exception was his middle finger, which was raised for weeks.

"I'd go to class and the professor would ask if anybody had a question and I would raise my hand with the middle finger sticking up," Clay recalled with a chuckle.

"One day I saw you hitchhiking to the North Campus, but nobody picked you up," I said.

"I guess they all thought I was flipping them off," Clay said.

In 1973, between semesters, Clay began working for the Penn Central railroad.

"I started out as a trackman," said Clay, who majored in business and lived in Westchester County, New York.

Around this time, he joined the Saint Michael's wind ensemble as a trombone player.

"Tim and Peter were in it, too," said Clay, who continued to play the instrument and work on the railroad after graduation.

"Conrail took over in 1976 and I got foreman's rights in 1977," he said, adding that he took a brief break from the trombone but picked it up again in the early 1980s.

"I was playing with marching bands and concert bands here and there," Clay said. "I stayed as a foreman with the railroad because if I became a supervisor, I'd be on twenty-four-hour call, so I decided to stick with music and figured that after I retired, I'd be able to do something with it. Thankfully, everything worked out that way."

In 2013, at age sixty, Clay retired from the railroad, which by that time was Metro-North.

"I could have retired at fifty-five, but I stuck it out until sixty to get the max," said Clay, who gets a railroad pension but not Social Security. "I had thirty years, which was the magic number. I'm blessed with the pension. I never paid into Social Security, but with the railroad retirement, I'm getting more."

The year before, Clay's wife, Lorraine, retired from a career that included jobs at a bank, a doctor's office, and a Swiss company that did automotive work.

Now she has her own herbology company, Empowered by Nature, in Dutchess County, New York, where she and Clay have taken up residence.

"When I was living in Westchester, I was playing in a big band in Harrison," said Clay. "One of the guys in the band also played in a group called the Big Band Sound. When I moved up to Dutchess, he introduced me to the band in 1995."

One of the band members was also playing at Marist College in Dutchess County. Marist had been invited to play at the 1998 Kickoff Classic, a college football game at the former Giants Stadium in East Rutherford, New Jersey.

"Florida State was playing Texas A&M," Clay recalled. "Florida State asked all the colleges in the area to go down to the Meadowlands. I jumped on a bus and went along. It was a great time. I was talking to the director of the Marist band, which had twenty-five students. He asked if I wanted to join, even though I wasn't a student. I said, 'Why not?'"

Clay played the trombone (and now plays the tuba, too, though not at the same time) but became instrumental in another way.

"One of the students dropped a baritone, which is a small tuba," he related. "The director asked if I would mind taking it home to get the dents out. I have always been handy, but I had no tools, so I got a two-by-four and hammered the bell out. Then I started repairing other instruments. I got repair tools, which are pretty expensive and only specific for each instrument. I did it out of my basement for quite a few years. In the summer I would take the instruments home in my truck, repair them in the basement, and take them back. Then Marist got a music building not long after I retired and they gave me a little repair shop. I've been doing that for five or six years."

Clay also has continued to play with the Big Band Sound, but now, in the age of coronavirus, he's rehearsing with the group every Wednesday night on Zoom.

"Retirement has been great," he told me. "You might even say it's music to my ears."

"The Office: The Final Episode"

Jim Smith, Liane Guenther, and Alan Fallick were among my Newsday co-workers, which is misleading because, while they did a lot of work, I worked at avoiding it.

It worked.

Nonetheless, we did some good stuff and had some good times, too. Now they, like me, are retired.

Jim Smith

Of the many friends I made at Newsday, Jim was the closest. That's literally true because we sat next to each other for years.

"I remember when you used to be funny," Jim would say, the trace of a smile under his steel-gray mustache, after I had made some typically inane remark.

Jim was a man I liked, admired, respected, and always, every day, on deadline or during a lull, joked around with.

He did the same with me. Once, after he and his wife, Lynn, returned from a trip to Florida, Jim told me that he was worried somebody was going to take his beach chair while he was swimming.

"I put one of your books on it," he deadpanned. "No one touched it."

Jim was at Newsday for forty-eight years, thirty-three as a sportswriter. He started as an apprentice on high school and college sports. Then he was on the pro football beat, covering the New York Giants for six years. After that, he was Newsday's hockey writer, covering the New York Islanders and Rangers for thirteen years.

Finally, for fifteen years, he was a copy editor, first on the sports desk, then in features, where he was stuck with me.

"Sitting next to you made it bearable," Jim said. "I couldn't have made it without the yucks from you. I was going through some rough times and you always put things in perspective."

I was so touched and so moved by those kind words that I paused for a moment to compose myself, took a deep breath, and said, "Is this the wrong number?"

"You idiot!" Jim bellowed into the phone.

We both laughed.

Jim always did good work at Newsday. Since retiring at age sixty-six on Dec. 31, 2014, he has been doing good works.

Actually, Jim has been socially conscious for as long as I have known him. But his time away from the job had long been filled with family responsibilities. He and Lynn have a son, Pete, a fine young man who works as an air-traffic controller.

Then there was his competitive passion: ice hockey. The hockey writer was still a hockey player long after he stopped covering the sport.

"I played six hundred and eighty-five games in twelve seasons," said Jim, referring to pick-up contests that often involved players who were far younger. "I had eight hundred and seventy goals, a thousand and fifty-six assists, and one thousand nine hundred and twenty-six points. Only Wayne Gretzky, at two thousand eight hundred and fifty-two, had more points than me. And that doesn't even include all the games I played before age fifty-four."

Jim was so "nuts," as he put it, that he played for seven years after having heart surgery. But two shoulder operations put an end to his career.

"Are you in the Hockey Hall of Fame?" I asked.

"No," Jim replied.

"There's no justice," I said.

But justice, of the social variety, is Jim's true passion.

His first big project after retiring from Newsday was to write a book about his experiences in Vietnam, where he was a reporter for Stars & Stripes, the U.S. Defense Department's daily newspaper.

"I saw every major city in Vietnam from the Delta to the Demilitarized Zone from 1971 to 1972," said Jim, whose book, "Heroes to the End: An Army Correspondent's Last Days in Vietnam," was published in 2015.

Jim has donated all his book-sale proceeds and speaking fees, which have amounted to more than twelve thousand dollars, to United Veterans Beacon House, a Long Island nonprofit that runs forty-seven homeless shelters for veterans and others. Beacon House sees that clients apply for and receive benefits, transports them for medical appointments, counsels them on mental health problems, and refers them out for issues such as traumatic brain injury and post-traumatic stress disorder.

Jim, who is vice president on the board of Beacon House, also is on the boards of ERASE Racism; a Port Washington, New York, post of the Veterans of Foreign Wars; and a group of eleven Unitarian Universalist congregations.

"My plate is pretty full," said Jim, adding: "During those fifteen years I was an editor, I laid the groundwork for retirement. I was on the church board that gave ten million dollars a year for my four years to progressive groups around the country. So my eyes were opened to inequality."

When he was an editor on the features copy desk, Jim wrote a short-lived but important column called "Giving Back."

He continues to give back every day but still finds time to enjoy retirement with Lynn, who retired from working for Nassau County, New York, as a therapist and is now in private practice.

"We have a good life," Jim said. "Before retirement, I was concerned about doing things for Jim Smith. Now I'm concerned about doing things for others."

Liane Guenther

At work, Liane was an editor. In retirement, she's a lady of the evening.

"Not that kind," Liane explained, much to my relief. "There are three of us: Genellen, Shelly, and me. We're neighbors and we call ourselves the Ladies of the Evening. We sit outside — at a social distance, of course — and have cocktails. It's one of the best things about retirement."

Liane was at Newsday, she said, "thirty-seven years, five months, and three days — not that I was counting."

When I was there, I was often asked, "Who's your boss?"

My patented response: "Who isn't?"

Liane was among my many supervisors over the years. She was the best: fair, funny, talented, patient, thoroughly professional, and Midwest (born in Nebraska, lived in Minnesota) nice.

Her last official title was senior features news editor.

"My son Max said he liked that title except for the 'senior' part," Liane recalled with a chuckle.

She and her husband, Bill, have another son, Will. He and Max are in their thirties and are wonderful and successful young men.

Bill, a talented Newsday photographer and a great, soft-spoken guy, took a buyout in 2010 at age sixty-four.

"He took retirement very seriously," Liane said. "He knew that once I retired, his retirement was over. We have a lot of projects he was ignoring for ten years. He was very successful. Bill promised but never delivered."

And now?

"Now," said Liane, "those projects are going to get done."

One is the twenty-two-foot sailboat that has been sitting in the driveway since 1997.

"It has not moved since then," Liane said. "It was Bill's intention to either sell the boat or paint the bottom and put it back in the water. Guess who's doing the work now."

Liane also has been busy selling furniture and other items for a friend's son who bought a nearby cottage.

"It's a small place, but it has the most amazing view," she said, adding that the owners died and the cottage, which has been vacant for two years, will be torn down.

"There's this amazing stuff — antiques, furniture, glassware, all kinds of things," said Liane. "My friend Judy called to ask if I would help clean out the house so they could tear it down."

One of the items was a century-old, solid oak upright piano.

"Two guys — and older man and a small, younger one — picked up the piano to put it on a dolly," Liane said. "The dolly went racing down the street toward the water."

"Was the piano on it?" I asked breathlessly.

"No, thank God," Liane reported. "But there are a million stories about this place. That's been one of the fun things I've done since I retired."

She also is forming a group of people who go to companies, hospitals, and other places and put together newsletters and annual reports.

"I've been working on that," Liane said. "And right now, Bill is painting our cast-iron lawn furniture." She laughed and added, "I've been keeping him busy."

Liane was sixty-eight when she took the buyout, though she stayed for a few more weeks to work on a special project.

"It was so much fun when you were there," she told me. "I always hated it when you were on vacation. It was so dull. You took your job seriously, you were a serious editor, but everything else was up for grabs."

"You were a fantastic boss," I said.

"I did love my staff," said Liane. "Everyone was terrific. But I retired at the right time. I thank God every day that Newsday offered the buyout and we had the good sense to take it. Journalism was great, but there's nothing like being a Lady of the Evening."

Alan Fallick

Alan was at Newsday, as he put it, "just shy of thirty-nine years, although I have never been shy."

"You were like Jack Benny," I said, referring to the legendary comedian who claimed, no matter his real age, to be thirty-nine years old.

"The difference," said Alan, "is that I'm still alive." He gave a Jack Benny pause. "At least I think so."

Alan started at Newsday in 1980 as a copy editor on the sports desk.

"It was a later shift," he remembered. "To help me get a feel for the way things worked, they also had me close pages in the composing room."

When he married Joy in 1992, he asked to work an earlier shift.

"I thought it would be nice if I got a day job," Alan said. "I became the copy chief on the regional daytime desk, which was great for me because I got to see my wife more." Another Benny pause. "I don't know if it was great for her."

Alan was responsible for eight regional zones of the paper, but in 1995 Newsday combined the regional desk with the features desk. Two years later, I arrived.

"When you got here," Alan said, "I applied to go to any other department." Pause. "I got stuck with you anyway."

Alan was an assistant news editor before becoming news editor on the features desk. Two years before he took the buyout, he went to the night news desk.

"After I retired, I went to Heckscher Park and ran into one of the paper's former artists," Alan recalled. "He told me about another colleague who had taken a prior buyout and had moved to New England. He said the other former colleague told him that the highlight of his day was going out to the mailbox. That resonated with me. I also spoke with a financial adviser who said, 'A lot of people your age and older need to have a purpose, a goal. If you retire and are just puttering around the house, those folks don't last long.' I remembered that."

Alan, who was sixty-seven when he retired, has been putting together the pieces to start a legacy video business.

"It would be for parents and grandparents, putting together family memories," Alan said. "I wasn't moving too fast on it, so I was just keeping it warm on the back burner. Then I went to Liane's farewell party, was asked about doing a part-time gig, and soon thereafter was offered a chance to work on the letters to the editor. I didn't think twice about it."

Alan and Joy, who have two adult daughters, Juliet and Laura, are both home. Joy, nine years younger than Alan, is a registered nurse medical claims reviewer and has worked remotely during the pandemic.

"My gig is always remote," Alan said. "They want me as far away from the office as possible."

Now that they're quarantined, he and Joy get to spend lots of time together.

"We both think it's perfect," said Alan. One last Jack Benny pause. "Well, I do."

CHAPTER 9

(The coronavirus pandemic has been no laughing matter, but I did manage to find humor in the quarantine, which also gave Sue an unexpected preview of life with me in retirement.)

"Diary of a Mad House Couple"

At the risk of being shot on sight, which is a possibility for me even under normal conditions, I am confined to my house with my lovely wife, Sue, who is beginning to wonder what would be worse: getting sick or being quarantined with me.

If you think you are bored out of your skull while confined to your house, too, read this diary.

Monday: Day one of the official hunkering down begins when Sue, a teacher's assistant, learns that school has been canceled indefinitely.

"My job has been canceled forever," I tell her.

"You're retired," she points out.

"That's why," I respond.

"What do you want to do?" Sue asks.

I wiggle my eyebrows. She rolls her eyeballs.

"Is that all you can think about?" she huffs.

"Of course not," I say. "Sometimes I think about hockey."

"My God," Sue sighs. "This is going to be hell."

Tuesday: We turn on the television to see medical experts (none of whom is a politician) tell us to wash our hands.

I go into the bathroom and follow orders. I lose count of the number of times I have lathered up, which works me into a lather because the total must exceed the population of Patagonia.

"We could have our own soap opera," I tell Sue.

She shakes her head sadly.

I paraphrase the Stealers Wheel song: "You're stuck in the house with me."

Sue goes to bed. Tomorrow will be another long day.

Wednesday: Sue says she has to go to the store for essentials.

"Beer and wine?" I ask.

"Soap and sanitizer," she replies.

"Buy some lotion, too," I say. "The skin on my hands is starting to peel off."

"The store may be out of it," Sue says.

"I hope not," I say. "At this rate, I'll bleed to death."

Sue takes wipes and gloves with her.

"Be careful," I say. "And don't breathe until you get back home."

Thursday: The situation is, of course, very serious. Tens of thousands are infected and many have already died. But I am starting to get really annoyed at newscasters and politicians who urge me to follow strict guidelines "out of an abundance of caution."

"As opposed to what?" I ask Sue. "A minimum of it?"

I also have noticed that everyone in the United States — except me — now has a medical degree. They're all experts in what I should or shouldn't do and do not hesitate to say that whatever I have been doing to stay safe is totally wrong.

I hope the real doctors find a vaccine soon.

Friday: It has been five days since Sue and I have been quarantined. While we have been happily married for almost forty-two years, we are starting to get on each other's nerves.

"Togetherness is nice," she says, "but there is such a thing as too much of it."

"Just wait until you're retired," I say.

"If this is what retirement will be like," Sue tells me, "I may have to get a part-time job."

"Get one in a liquor store," I say. "We're almost out of wine."

Saturday: I go to the pharmacy to pick up a prescription. The pharmacist is wearing a mask.

"Are you robbing the place?" I ask her.

She smiles (I think) and says, "No. This is out of an abundance of caution."

I stifle a scream, pay for the medicine, and make a beeline out of there.

Sunday: I tell Sue that we can't go to church.

"We haven't gone in years," she reminds me.

Instead, we give each other the sign of peace and share a kiss.

"We're pretty lucky," I say.

"Yes, we are," Sue replies sweetly. "Now wash your hands."

"The Great American Grandfather"

Dan Patrick
Lieutenant Governor
Austin, Texas

Dear Lt. Gov. Patrick:

I'm Jerry Zezima, a fellow grandfather who has five grandchildren, all of whom are more mature than I am.

I'm writing in response to your suggestion that grandparents sacrifice themselves in the wake of this terrible pandemic to get the economy going again.

I want you to know that I am a proud American who loves this country more than anything except — you guessed it — my grandchildren.

Still, I am willing to do my part to help the economy. It's something I have always done. Look at the facts: I have been in excellent health my whole life, especially in the past thirty years, a stretch in which the economy has boomed more than at any time in our nation's history.

Coincidence? I think not.

As my doctor will tell you, I had a bad cold in 2008 and look what happened. That's right: the Great Recession. Now I admit that this virus is far worse than a case of the sniffles. And how a recession could be called great is beyond my addled geezer brain to understand.

But you need to understand that if I sacrificed myself, in a foolhardy move that would undoubtedly be known as Zexit, the economic structure of the United States, and possibly the entire world, would collapse like a grandfather chasing a toddler.

Speaking of the little ones, what would become of them if we grandparents violated the code of social distancing and started sneezing on each other, leading to our inevitable demise? Aside from the fact that their parents (our children) wouldn't have to care for us in our old age, which in my case, according to my daughters, arrived years ago, they would be devastated.

People who are willing to talk to me, which narrows the field considerably, have often asked if I spoil my grandchildren.

"No," I tell them. "That's my wife's job. My job is to corrupt them."

And if I may be permitted to brag a bit, I do it better than any grandfather in this great country of ours. No offense, Lt. Gov. Patrick, but that includes you.

Here are some examples of how the corruption of my grandchildren has made them happy, healthy young people who will grow up to be productive citizens — the kind of driven, hardworking Americans who will follow my selfless lead in creating a robust economy.

In an outstanding patriotic gesture, I took my eldest grandchild, Chloe, who was two years old at the time, to the White House Easter Egg Roll. It was during the administration of the previous president, which probably doesn't score points with you, but I stood in line longer than it takes Congress to pass an economic stimulus bill just so Chloe could meet not the commander-in-chief, but her hero, Peppa Pig.

If memory serves (I'd like it to serve me a beer right now), the stock market zoomed the next day.

I took my grandson Xavier to the Smithsonian. I'm surprised I wasn't put on exhibit, but it was another patriotic gesture that benefited a great American institution.

I've taken the kids bowling. We've gone to the zoo. I've bought them ice cream and doughnuts. All of these outings have pumped money into the economy.

And don't forget my wife, Sue, the children's grandmother. She has spent the fortune I'll never have on clothes and toys. It's helped the economy more than any stimulus bill ever could.

I trust that you understand why it would be a bad idea for me to sacrifice myself, Lt. Gov. Patrick. If you want to do it, go right ahead. Just give me the names of your grandchildren, who I am sure will miss you, and I will corrupt them, too.

Sincerely,
Jerry Zezima

"What's the Good Word?"

As a man of many words, not all of them repeatable in a quarantine, I will say that "quarantine" would be a great word to use if you were playing Scrabble.

That's because it would be worth 19 points, most of them coming from the letter Q, which by itself is worth 10. And if you got a triple word score, it would be worth 57 points.

Unfortunately, I didn't get enough of the right letters to spell "quarantine" during a game of Scrabble that Sue and I played when it became sadly apparent that there was nothing else to do while we were quarantined.

You might think that because I'm a writer, I would be a great Scrabble player. Not so. Sue, a teacher's assistant in a preschool, was an English major in college, where I, then a man of few words ("Another beer, bartender"), majored in stupidity.

My chances were slim (6 points) because I always lost when I played Sue's late grandmother. (She was alive then, which gave her an unfair advantage.) I was even defeated by Katie and Lauren when they were adolescents.

This was embarrassing (17 points), which is why I hadn't played Scrabble in years (8 points).

But on a rainy afternoon, after we got tired of watching HGTV (no points because acronyms and proper names aren't allowed), Sue suggested we engage in a war of words.

"Let's have some wine," said Sue, who had a glass of white (11 points) while I had a glass of red (only 4 points).

We sat at the kitchen table with the board and tiles.

"You go first," I told Sue, who replied, "You're such a gentleman."

"That would be worth 12 points," I remarked.

Sue took a sip of wine and said, "This is going to be a long game."

Her first word was "hand," which was worth 8 points.

Mine was "ham," which also was worth 8 points.

"It describes you," Sue commented.

Back and forth we went, up and down the board, trying for big scores with letters such as X (8 points), which Sue used to spell "fix" (13 points), and Z (10 points), which I used to spell "zonk" (17 points).

"Don't cheat by making up words," Sue said when I came up with something that is not, technically, English.

After Sue spelled "harp" (9 points), I added an O to make "Harpo," one of the Marx Brothers, but Sue immediately nixed it by saying it's a proper name.

"Imagine the score I could have had with Zeppo," I noted.

The game dragged on, with short, safe, low-impact words such as "mutt" (6 points), "dire" (5 points), and "gun" (4 points).

"Is 'ya' a word?" Sue asked.

"Ya," I responded.

It garnered Sue a grand total of 5 points.

"I'm out of vowels," she said.

"You can buy a vowel," I told her.

"That's on 'Wheel of Fortune,' not in Scrabble," Sue reminded me. "Besides, who would get the money?"

"Who else is here?" I said.

"Forget it," Sue said. "Your turn."

The game continued. So did the wine. Our battle (8 points) lasted so long that we each had a second glass.

"This is the only way the words 'Chardonnay' and 'Cabernet' are allowed in Scrabble," I said.

"Cheers," Sue replied.

Words such as "wet" (6 points), "trim" (6 points), and "lob" (5 points) appeared on the board before we ran out of tiles and the game was over.

Final score: Jerry 266, Sue 222.

"You wouldn't have won if my grandmother had been playing," Sue said.

I nodded and said, "You took the words right out of my mouth."

"Love at the Landfill"

Love, as a newfangled saying goes, means never having to say you're sorry for practicing social distancing.

Sue and I, who have always believed in social togetherness, celebrated our forty-second anniversary in the most romantic way possible in this age of quarantine:

We got out of the house and took a trip to the dump.

Our passion burned intensely as we contemplated a pile of logs that would never burn intensely in our backyard fire pit.

So, after they were cut up from a tree that was struck by lightning, which did not create sparks between us, Sue and I decided to load the logs into my car for a scenic drive to a nearby landfill.

While Sue, wearing gloves and a scarf, was at the grocery store to buy our pre-made anniversary dinners (spaghetti and clams for me, calamari for her), I was in the yard, plopping wood into a wheelbarrow.

At the same time, three cable guys showed up to do fiberoptic work.

"You couldn't have picked a better day," I told them. "It's my anniversary. And I'm celebrating by taking my wife to the landfill."

"Are they open?" the crew chief asked.

"Yes," I replied. "Just for me and my wife."

"That's so nice of them!" another guy exclaimed.

"Do they have champagne and strawberries for you?" a third one inquired.

"I hope so," I said before asking the crew chief if he was married.

"Yes," he said.

"Have you ever done anything this romantic with your wife?" I queried.

"No, you got me beat," he said.

When I told one of the other guys that Sue gave me the wheelbarrow for our anniversary a few years ago, he said, "What did she get for you this year, a shovel?"

Just then, Sue arrived back home.

"Happy anniversary!" the guys said to her in unison.

"Thank you!" Sue gushed.

"Are you going to the dump now?" one of them asked.

"Yes," said Sue.

"Do you have a picnic basket and a blanket?" the crew chief asked.

"That would have been a great idea — lunch at the landfill," I said.

"Have fun, you lovebirds!" the crew chief said as he and the other guys again wished us a happy anniversary and headed for the yard next door.

Sue and I put roughly seventeen tons of logs into the back of my car. As we buckled up in the front seat, I said, "You can't say I'm a bump on a log today."

Sue sighed and said, "Just drive."

When we got to the dump, I told the lady in the booth about our special day.

"It's our anniversary and we're spending it here," I said.

"Well," she responded, "it's a unique way to celebrate."

After parking in the designated area for brush and wood, we met a nice guy named Tony, who was unloading logs from his car, too.

"I don't know if I would bring my wife to the dump for our anniversary," he said, "but she does help me with yard work."

Tony helped Sue and me by taking a picture of us.

"It'll be a keepsake," he said. "You'll always remember your anniversary at the landfill."

Sue and I thanked Tony and drove home. We had so much fun that we loaded the car with more logs and made a second trip to the dump, where I told another booth attendant about this landmark event.

"Happy anniversary!" she said.

It was happy indeed. After Sue and I got back home, we had a candlelight dinner and toasted each other with wine.

"I don't know how we can top this next year," I said.

"I do," said Sue. "You can take me on a trip. And not to the dump."

"Hair Today, Gone Tomorrow"

To say that the quarantine has been hair-raising would be the unkindest cut of all. I know this because I hadn't had a haircut in a month and a half and was starting to look like Medusa, the mythical monster with snakes coming out of her head, so I risked shear hell and gave myself a trim.

On the plus side, I found out from my barber, Maria Santos, that my natural hair color is blond.

"Dirty blond," Maria said when I called her for a consultation in which she advised against using a hedge trimmer on my unruly locks, which were starting to sprout more gray matter than I have on the inside of my head.

Maria is to dye for. That's what she does when I go for a haircut. At my age (old enough to know better), I need a little touch-up to prevent me from looking like the geezer I really am.

The good news is that sixty-six is the new forty-six. The bad news is that I haven't looked forty-six since I was thirty-six.

At that age, I sported an Afro. I looked like legendary musician Billy Preston, whose massive mane probably prevented him from fitting through doorways.

I also resembled legendary comedian Harpo Marx, who had dirty blond curls and didn't speak, a characteristic that family, friends, and even complete strangers wish I would adopt.

"If you are going to cut your own hair," Maria said, "get a pair of professional hair-cutting scissors."

The problem, she added, is that if I ordered them online, they might not be delivered for weeks, at which point I'd need a landscaper.

When I asked about an electric hair clipper, which I also would have to order, Maria said, "If you start buzzing and make your hair too short, it could be a disaster."

"Then I'd look like Curly of the Three Stooges," I said. "Nyuk, nyuk, nyuk!"

"You could always wear a do-rag," Maria suggested.

"All I have is a don't-rag," I replied.

I decided to use a pair of regular household scissors, which I didn't tell Maria about because she had already warned me that in the wrong hands (mine), they also could cause trouble.

"Your hair is coarse," she explained.

"Maybe I could sell the clippings to Brillo," I said.

But I did tell her that I had bought a popular men's hair color product that, in my case, should be renamed Just for Morons.

"What shade did you get?" Maria asked.

"Medium brown," I answered.

"That's too dark," she said, adding that I should have gotten something lighter.

"I've always been lightheaded," I told Maria.

"That's because you're a dirty blond," she said.

"Do dirty blonds have more fun?" I wondered.

"Yes, but only if they don't mess up the color," said Maria, who added that leaving it in for five minutes, as recommended on the box, was excessive. "Men are impatient anyway," she said. "And you still want a little gray to show through so you can look distinguished."

I thanked Maria for her expertise and told her I'd make an appointment when it's safe to come out again. Then I went upstairs to the bathroom and, scissors in hand, took a little off the sides and around the ears. Fortunately, I didn't end up looking like Vincent van Gogh.

I applied the hair color to my head, mustache, and eyebrows, waited three minutes, and washed it out in the shower.

"Not bad," said Sue.

"I should open my own salon, Mr. Jerry's House of Style," I said.

"Don't even think about cutting my hair," Sue said.

"I can't wait until the quarantine is over," I said. "It sure has been a hairy situation."

"Look Who's Walking"

For years, countless people, many of whom I can't count on, have told me to take a hike. Now that we've been quarantined in a house where social distancing is impossible, unless you stay in the bathroom all day, Sue has been telling me to take one, too.

So I went on what I thought would be a leisurely stroll with her and almost ended up being a dead man walking.

That's because Sue is a power walker. I'm more like a Johnnie Walker. In fact, I should have scotched the walk as soon as it became apparent, approximately three yards into it, that I could never keep up without suffering some sort of cardiac event.

"It's a nice day," Sue said. "I need to get out or I'll go stir crazy."

"If you don't stir anything," I replied helpfully, "you won't go crazy."

Sue rolled her eyes and said, "Let's go."

And go we did, often at a pace that must have exceeded our neighborhood's speed limit of thirty miles an hour.

"You're going to get a ticket," I yelled as Sue zipped down the street.

If this had been the Kentucky Derby, in which I'd be the back end of a horse, Sue would have won going away.

"I can't keep up with you furlong," I said to Sue, who either couldn't hear me or refused to acknowledge the kind of remark that made her want to get out of the house in the first place.

Unlike racehorses, we weren't running, though I would have had to sprint to keep up with Sue, whose legs are much shorter than mine but evidently work like pistons, whereas mine operate more like the hands of a broken clock.

I knew our jaunt was dangerous when I saw her blow through two stop signs.

"Is that the way you drive?" I shouted.

Sue jammed on the brakes and idled at a third stop sign so I could catch up.

"Thanks," I said, gasping so violently that I was surprised I didn't inhale a passing Chihuahua, which was walking with a larger dog and two human companions.

"Hello!" I said. "It's a lovely day, isn't it?"

They ignored me and kept going.

"They're not practicing social distancing," I told Sue.

"They're probably married," she responded.

"The dogs?" I said.

Sue sighed and said, "On the next leg, we're going down this street and around the corner. Can you keep up?"

"If not, I'll die trying," I answered, having recovered enough to give up on the idea of pulling out my cellphone and calling 911.

Sue took off like a drag racer, which made me realize that behind every good woman is a man who's about to have a heart attack.

I stopped in front of a nice Colonial, not just to catch my breath, which must have smelled awful, but to let the operator of an SUV make a left turn into his driveway.

"I didn't want to collapse in front of your car," I told the guy, who had rolled down his window.

"Then you would have been a speed bump," he said with a smile as he pulled in.

I almost ended up being one anyway as I followed Sue, who was crossing the double yellow lines in the middle of the road. Cars that didn't come near her seemed to be aiming for me.

I imagined my obituary: "Elderly man becomes roadkill."

Finally, around the bend, what did I see? Our house! Sue, a former Girl Scout, stopped at the corner and helped me cross the street.

"We killed an hour," she said.

"You almost killed me," I replied.

Inside, I went to the refrigerator for a beer. It was the safest walk of the day.

"How to Wash Your Hands"

If, at the end of this pandemic, the world is hit with a biblical drought, which means there won't be enough water to make beer, there will be only one person to blame.

That would be yours truly. And the reason is simple: I wash my hands approximately a hundred and forty-seven times a day.

I also throw potentially contaminated jeans, pants, sweatpants, shirts, sweatshirts, T-shirts, boxer shorts, socks, pajamas, face masks, hand towels, bath towels, dish towels, dishcloths, washcloths, handkerchiefs, and anything else made of a washable material in the laundry at a rate that will undoubtedly cause a flood during the rinse cycle and the washing machine to sink like the Titanic.

But doctors, nurses, and other medical experts, who do not include politicians, even though some of them think they are, say it's important to wash your hands. This not only kills germs, but it can dry out your hands so much that you need to keep washing them to get the moisture necessary to dry them out again.

I have washed my hands so often that I am convinced one of two things will happen: (a) they will fall off, in which case I will either starve to death or be known as Stumpy, or (b) my skin will become so leathery that I will be classified as a reptile, which will give my wife an excuse to say, "See you later, alligator," or it will peel away in sheets and be used to make jackets, boots, and whips, in which case I will be known as Kinky.

Still, handwashing is *de rigueur mortis*, a French phrase meaning "socially required dead skin."

According to the aforementioned experts, and possibly the music industry, you should sing "Happy Birthday" to yourself twice while washing your hands. Unless you sing either too fast or too slowly, or can't remember the lyrics, or even your own name, this will take twenty seconds, which is how long it takes to eradicate the germs.

But according to those very same experts, who just won't shut up, most people wash their hands incorrectly because they don't get enough soap between their fingers and under their nails.

Also, when you wash your hands, you are supposed to go all the way up to your elbows. The third or fourth time I did this, because I don't catch on too quickly, it dawned on me that maybe I should roll up my sleeves.

But why stop at your elbows? Why not your armpits (which could probably use some soap) or your shoulders? Hell, why not strip naked and get in the shower? (Hint: Turn on the water or it won't work.)

But here's the real question: What if you wash your hands for only nineteen seconds? I guess that means it won't work, either, and you'll have to begin all over again.

One good thing to come out of this, aside from the fact that I should get a birthday cake every day, is that I sing so badly that even if I were around people other than my wife, it would ensure six feet (and maybe six miles) of social distancing.

One of the bad things is that if you go out, you have to wear gloves to keep your hands clean, but when you take them off, you have to wash your hands again. And you're not supposed to touch your face except, I suppose, to wash it, after which you should — that's right — wash your hands.

So it's a good idea to listen to the experts, even at the risk of creating a worldwide water shortage.

And after this pandemic is over, I am going to wash my hands of the whole damn thing.

"Just What the Doctor Ordered"

If I have learned anything during this pandemic, aside from the fact that it's extremely difficult to eat while wearing a face mask, making starvation another health risk, it's that having a good doctor is very important.

I also have learned that it's not a good idea to go to the doctor because you could get sick. Then, of course, you'd have to go to the doctor.

That's why I was happy to see my doctor without having to leave the house.

I used my cellphone to have a virtual visit with Dr. M, which stands for mirth because he believes that laughter is the best medicine, not to mention the cheapest, even with a copay.

He proved it by telling me a joke that's too risqué to repeat here. It involved dogs.

"You're not even a veterinarian," I told Dr. M.

"It doesn't matter," he said. "It was a good joke."

"Are you going to prescribe flea powder?" I asked.

"No," he said. "Just dog biscuits."

"How do I look?" I wondered.

"Very healthy," Dr. M said.

"I always look better from a distance," I noted.

"Are you more than six feet away?" the good doctor asked.

"Try about three miles," I said.

"Good," he said. "That means you don't have to wear a mask."

"Should I stick out my tongue and say 'ah'?" I wanted to know.

"Did you brush your teeth?" he asked.

"This morning," I said. "Or was it yesterday morning?"

"Don't bother," said Dr. M, who told me that his medical assistant, Jennifer, was going to ask me some questions.

She popped up on the screen wearing a mask, through which she said, "Hi, Mr. Zezima." Then she said, "How tall are you?"

"I'm sitting down, so I'm about three-foot-eight," I replied.

"How tall are you when you're standing up?" Jennifer asked.

"Six feet," I said. "But I need a haircut, so I'm probably more like six-five."

"How much do you weigh?" Jennifer asked.

"I had a big lunch, so I feel like I'm four hundred pounds," I said. "Ordinarily, I'm one seventy-five."

"How old are you?" Jennifer inquired.

"According to Social Security, I'm sixty-six," I said.

"You don't look it," said Jennifer.

"You mean I look even older?" I said. "I must be having a bad face day."

"You're a young man," said Dr. M, who is older than I am.

I rolled up my sleeve, extended my arm, and asked, "Are you going to take my blood pressure?"

"We haven't figured out how to do that through the computer," he said. "But you seem to have a pulse. How are you doing in this pandemic?"

"Fine, except I'm bothered by two things," I said. "First, everyone tells me that everything I'm doing to stay safe is wrong. They think they're all experts."

"Tell them to call me," said Dr. M. "What's the other thing?"

"Those TV commercials for medicines that are supposed to help you, but they come with warnings about how bad they can be," I said. "Some of the side effects include death."

"If a medicine can kill you," Dr. M said, "don't take it. Water is good for you, but if you are under it, you can drown. If it's too hot, it can kill you. If it's too cold, it can kill you. Everything in moderation. Have a glass of red wine at dinner. It's good for the heart."

"You have a very good phone-side manner," I said.

"Thank you," Dr. M replied. "And I didn't keep you waiting."

"My time is not valuable," I said, "but I appreciate it."

"Stay healthy," Dr. M said before signing off, "and you'll always have the last laugh."

"Here's the Dirt on Vegetables"

Jerry, Jerry, quite contrary, how does your garden grow?

Not too well, unfortunately, because my green thumb is probably a fungus and Sue is the real gardener in the family. I just provide the fertilizer.

But since the weather was nice and we wanted to get out of the house, where Sue has been stuck with me since the quarantine began, I decided to help start her garden, where she will grow all the vegetables I don't like but have to eat anyway because, as Sue often tells me, "they're good for you."

To which I invariably reply, "I'm a vegetable myself. Isn't that good enough?"

Apparently not, so Sue and I went to the landfill to get free topsoil.

"It's even better than dirt cheap," I said as I shoveled the stuff into two large lawn and garden bags, which weighed so much that lifting them into the car was a pain in the asparagus.

When we got home, I unloaded the loam, sweet loam and went to the shed, a dilapidated structure housing tools that, to call a spade a spade, I hate. That's because they are dangerous weapons in my hands, which often bleed as a result, and are used to grow the vegetables I hate even more.

One of the tools I brought out looked like a spade, but Sue corrected me.

"That's an ice chopper!" she said incredulously. "Wrong season. A lot you know about planting a garden."

I knew enough to bring out more appropriate tools, including a shovel, a hoe, a leaf rake, an iron rake, and a trowel.

I ripped open the bags of soil and dumped them into the garden, a small patch measuring ten feet by five feet in which Sue planned to plant beets, onions, string beans, peppers, basil, cucumbers, and, with apologies to Simon and Garfunkel, parsley, sage, rosemary, and thyme.

She also will grow tomatoes, which I like because botanically they aren't vegetables but fruits, and squash, which I dislike more than anything that grows in nature with the possible exception of poison ivy, though it probably tastes better.

"Why don't you like squash?" Sue asked.

"Because," I replied, "I'd rather play tennis."

Sue rolled her eyes, through which she noticed that I was standing there, a shovel in one hand, an iron rake in the other, like one half of the famous Grant Wood painting "American Gothic."

"Are you the Farmer in the Dell?" Sue asked.

"I'm more like the Farmer in the Dull," I responded.

Sue didn't disagree.

"Or," I added, "if you pickle the cucumbers, I'd be the Farmer in the Dill."

Sue ignored the remark and said, "Last year, I had red hot chili peppers."

"I must have missed the concert," I noted.

"I put them in the freezer," Sue said.

"I guess they're not hot anymore," I told her.

She told me to get going, which meant using the leaf rake to remove leftover autumn leaves, the shovel to dig up clumps of dead grass, and the iron rake to spread out the dirt.

Then Sue got down and dirty as she planted rows of onion and beet seeds.

"Do you want me to help?" I asked. "I've gone to seed."

Sue declined my generous offer but warned me to watch out for her chamomile flowers.

"The chamomile fits you to a tea," I said.

"Too bad I can't plant grapes," Sue remarked. "I'd use them to make wine. After being out here with you, I need a glass."

Still, it was a successful start to the garden, where Sue will grow all the greens that are supposedly good for me.

"Thanks," I said as I put away the tools. "Now I can throw in the trowel."

"Hollywood, Here We Come"

If you happen to be watching the next Oscars telecast, don't be surprised if you see me up on the stage, holding a golden statuette, thanking the Academy, joking with Steven Spielberg, and, in my best Sally Field voice, crying, "You like me! You really like me!"

Even though I can't leave the house during this pandemic to do much more than take out the garbage, I've gone Hollywood.

My entertainment career began when, as a retiree who was bored out of my skull, which is empty anyway, I signed up to be an extra in movies and TV shows.

The casting agencies that get jobs for "background actors" (or, as we are known in the business, "talent," which in my case is in short supply) started sending me notices about upcoming opportunities.

One was a gig in which I would have played a corpse in one of the three hundred and fifty-two cop shows currently airing, streaming, crawling, or whatever these programs do nowadays.

Sue said I would be a natural. I wanted to take it as a compliment.

"I'd have to hold my breath for a long time," I said. "I could end up being an actual corpse. But at least I'd be a star."

"Don't hold your breath," Sue responded.

I was scheduled to go for an interview in New York City with one of the agencies when the industry shut down, partly because of the quarantine and partly, I am sure, to prevent me from totally ruining show business.

But that didn't stop me from pursuing my dream of rubbing shoulders with Tom Hanks and Meryl Streep, who would probably have me arrested for rubbing shoulders with them.

So I started making videos.

At first, I didn't know what I was doing. At second, I didn't know what I was doing. But as Ed Harris's character said in "Apollo 13," which was directed by Ron Howard, "Failure is not an option."

(Ron, who was wonderfully sweet to Lauren when she worked at a coffee shop in Stamford many years ago, is my fourth-favorite Hollywood Howard, the first three being Shemp, Moe, and Curly.)

I used my cellphone to record the first of my "Quarantine Update" videos, this one about how poor Sue is stuck in the house with me and how we have passed the time by playing Scrabble. I was the screenwriter, the cinematographer, the director, and, of course, the star.

I did the same on my next three videos (about relaxing in a hammock, cutting my own hair, and taking a walk), but I enlisted Sue to direct my fifth video (about washing my hands).

All five videos are on YouTube, where they can be viewed by movie lovers who also are bored silly with the quarantine.

That includes Sue, a teacher's assistant who has, with my directorial help, made several of her own videos for her school's remote classroom lessons. She's a natural. I'm an unnatural. Together, we could be Hollywood's new power couple.

I can see us now, at the Academy Awards, strutting our stuff on the red carpet, Sue in a snazzy black tuxedo, me in a shimmering gown, smiling for the paparazzi and signing autographs for adoring fans.

My production company, DumbWorks, will get credit for the armload of Oscars Sue and I will take back to our PVC-gated mansion, where the statuettes will stand proudly on top of the refrigerator, which contains the beer we will drink to celebrate our success.

Even after the quarantine is over, we will continue to make videos because we are, after all, artists.

All right, Mr. Spielberg, I'm ready for my close-up.

"A Pie-in-the-Sky Idea"

When the moon hits the sky like a big pizza pie, that's a-boring.

And that's why Sue, desperate for a diversion during the quarantine, asked me to help her make pizza.

"I'm bored out of my mind," she explained, apparently not bothered by the fact that her husband, who has been driving her crazy while she's been cooped up in the house all these weeks, has been out of his mind for the entire forty-two years of our marriage.

Sue has made pizza before, and it's always been delicious, but this was the first time she had asked me for a hand.

"How about two hands?" I offered.

Sue shook her head and said, "I have a feeling this is going to be a mistake."

She had already taken out five pita breads that would substitute for pizza dough.

"I guess I can't twirl them in the air like they do in pizzerias," I said.

"Not unless you want to hit the ceiling fan," replied Sue, pointing out that the fan was on and the bread would go flying across the kitchen and possibly hit me in the eye like a big pizza pie.

"That would be amore," I said, snuggling up to Sue.

"Keep your mind on your work," she ordered.

The work involved making five pies: tomato and basil; red and green peppers, onions, black olives, and tomatoes; sausage, peppers, and onions; sausage, peppers, onions, and mushrooms; and sausage and mushrooms.

"I ran out of meatballs," said Sue, who usually makes my favorite, meatballs and spinach.

"That's Popeye's favorite, too," I pointed out.

Since Sue couldn't roll her dough, she rolled her eyes.

"Make yourself useful," she told me.

"What do you want me to do?" I asked, afraid she would answer, "Get lost."

She didn't. Instead, she said, "Slice the olives."

They were small and the knife was large, but I managed to succeed without slicing off a finger.

"That would be quite a topping, wouldn't it?" I remarked.

Sue ignored it and said, "Now slice the tomatoes."

I did, after which I sliced the mushrooms and some of the peppers and onions, the last of which, I said, "can make a grown man cry."

Sue looked like she was about to burst into tears when I told her I would sprinkle the ingredients, which I had helped her brown in a pan on the stove, over the pita breads.

"I asked you to help, not take over," Sue said as I also used a tablespoon to spread canned pizza sauce on the breads, which I then topped with, of course, the toppings.

"Now sprinkle on the cheese," Sue said, handing me a bag of shredded Romano, a fistful of which I shoved, along with a few toppings, into my mouth.

"Stop eating the ingredients!" she commanded.

Finally, the five pizzas were ready to be put into the oven.

"They look good," I said.

When they came out twenty minutes later, they tasted good.

"Yum!" I exclaimed as I stuffed my face with a slice of the pie with sausage, peppers, and onions.

"It came out pretty well," Sue said, adding: "These days I have nothing else to do but cook. I'm bored. I don't know how I am going to retire."

I've been retired for months; Sue, a teacher's assistant, has been working remotely while school has been closed due to the pandemic.

"Maybe," I suggested, "we can open our own pizza joint, with curbside service. I can see it now: Jerry and Sue's."

"Sue and Jerry's," Sue said. "And you can't take over my creations."

"All right," I said as I took another bite. "But we do make a good pizza team. Any way you slice it."

"A Houseboy Comes Clean"

When it comes to housework, my wife has it maid. And she is not too proud to say that the maid is her husband.

Maybe it's because I don't have a little French maid's dress, which I would happily wear except I can't find one in my size and I'd probably fall down while vacuuming in high heels, but I am one step up from being a domestic worker.

I am, according to my wife, a houseboy.

"That's your title," said Sue, who has told countless people of my new role in the family hierarchy.

To which Lauren commented: "It's better than being a pool boy."

If I were, I'd have to be a kiddie pool boy, because that is where Chloe and Lilly like to frolic. Besides, on a maid's salary, which amounts to exactly zero, it's the only kind of pool I can afford.

Still, for the first four-plus decades of my marriage, I had been practically useless around the house. But ever since I retired several months ago, and especially now, during the quarantine, when Sue could see how good a job I do, I have aspired to be a centerfold in Good Housekeeping.

As I have told Sue, "A husband's work is never done."

And it takes a lot of it to keep our humble abode clean enough to pass the white glove test. Unfortunately, I don't have a pair of white gloves, which would get ruined in the toilet anyway, so I use rubber ones. They keep my delicate hands smooth and young-looking.

Speaking of the toilet, I am flush with excitement to say that the bathroom is where I shine. Since the Ty-D-Bol man is no longer with us, I have taken his place, though I can't fit a motor boat in the porcelain convenience. A good thing, too, because otherwise I'd go down the tubes.

Nonetheless, I do a sparkling job, if I do say so myself. Sue has said it as well, especially after I injured my back while bending down to clean the floor behind the toilet.

She wasn't so happy when I used what I thought was an old toothbrush to scrub the chrome faucet on the sink.

"That was my new one!" Sue protested.

"Sorry," I apologized. "Want to use mine?"

"No!" she shot back.

Picky, picky.

At least Sue never complains about my vacuuming, which leaves our carpets and rugs free of dirt, lint, and whatever else gathers underfoot. Speaking of feet, I once caught my big toe in the vacuum cleaner while wearing flip-flops. Now I make sure to don heavier footwear.

Sue also likes how I dust, especially when I use the dusting wand to reach high places, where I don't have friends but do have bookshelves and ceiling-fan blades.

"Let's not get into a dust-up," I once said.

"If you don't watch out," Sue replied, "unto dust you shall return."

I sweep the kitchen floor (and try to sweep Sue off her feet), wash the dishes (dishes my life), iron clothes (I am, after all, a member of the press), clean windows (it's a pane in the neck), and do just about everything else except laundry. That's because Sue doesn't trust me. She thinks I'll either flood the place or break the washing machine.

"Life is a vicious cycle," I told her.

"Pick up your dirty socks and underwear," she said.

"Too bad I don't have a little French maid's dress," I said. "You'd have to wash that, too."

"If you clean the house, it'll be worth it," Sue said.

"I'll go shopping for one tomorrow," I said. "I hope there's a sale on fishnet stockings."

"It's Not the Heat, It's the Stupidity"

Because I am full of hot air, which could earn me a spot as a float in the Macy's Thanksgiving Day Parade, I have learned not to sweat the small stuff.

Instead, I save it for the big stuff, like installing air conditioners, which works me into such a sweat that I need to turn them on immediately so I won't pop like a helium balloon and go flying out the window.

That's why this year, like the previous twenty-one years we have been in our house, Sue and I have vowed to get central air-conditioning next year.

"This is the last time I'm doing this," I told Sue as we headed for the storage area of the garage, where I dumped the bedroom and office air conditioners after I took them out of their respective windows last year.

"You're too old," Sue stated.

"I am not," I responded defensively, even though I am clearly a geezer. "I just don't want to wrench my back like I did a few years ago and end up looking like Quasimodo. I have a hunch it will happen again."

This was the worst year because we rearranged the storage area to make room for a new refrigerator, with the result that the two air conditioners were buried under and surrounded by so much stuff that, if it were put on a scale at a truck stop, the stuff would have outweighed the air conditioners.

And trust me, each unit weighs approximately as much as a baby grand piano, which I can't even play.

Since we have been waiting during the quarantine for a new kitchen cabinet to be installed, the stuff included enough dishes to feed the entire population of Liechtenstein if we invited them over for dinner. For this and other reasons that made no sense, there also were coffee cups, soup bowls, a sugar bowl, three chairs, a large metal pot, toilet paper, popcorn, a stool, board games, paper towels, Christmas lights,

Easter baskets, a wreath, several tote bags, and a big plastic bin filled with Christmas decorations.

"You can maneuver your way around this stuff," Sue said.

"I can't maneuver around you," I said as she stood in my way.

"You're always looking for the easy way out," Sue replied.

"There is no easy way out of this," I noted as we cleared a path.

With each unit, I squatted, tried to get a firm grasp, gritted my teeth, and, with a jerk (me), rose to my feet, one of which, I was sure, would be flattened like roadkill if I dropped the metal monstrosity.

Through the garage, the laundry room, the kitchen, the family room, and the front hallway I lurched, resting at the bottom of the stairs before climbing the domestic equivalent of Mount Everest.

It was a miracle I didn't rupture a vital organ.

I got the bedroom AC in the window, which I took the precaution to open first, but had to take it back out when Sue noticed that it was resting so precariously on the sill that it would undoubtedly wait until I was outside, directly underneath, before falling two stories onto my skull, which wouldn't faze me but would damage the unit so badly that I'd have to buy a new one.

I repeated this process with the office AC, the installation of which required me to move a bookcase — after taking out all the books, of course — so I could plug the stupid thing in.

Both are working nicely, making the upstairs comfortable for sleeping and working, which I often do simultaneously, but this time I mean it: Next year, we're getting central air.

"If not," I told Sue, "I will definitely lose my cool."

"Where There's a Grill, There's a Way"

When it comes to grilling, I am usually cooking with gas. Unfortunately, I couldn't cook on our new grill for a month after we bought it. And even with the gas off, I almost blew my top.

The hot-button issue began when Sue and I went to a home improvement store for a new grill to replace our old one, a pathetic contraption we had for several years, during which time it charred countless hamburgers, hot dogs, spareribs, and (yuck!) vegetables. Eventually, rust and grease were the words.

So Sue and I got a new grill that would be delivered already assembled. A good thing, too, because I put together the first grill we ever had. It took me a week. When I finally got it assembled, there were about a dozen parts left over.

Like a mobster who makes his wife start his car every morning, I told Sue that if she wanted me to cook on the grill, she'd have to light it.

Luckily, we didn't have a blowup. All the grills we've had since then have come pre-assembled.

That included this latest one, which was delivered about two weeks after we bought it. The problem was that, unlike the others, it wouldn't start. At first I thought it was the tank, so I bought a new one with, of course, fresh gas, which is frequently the result of my cooking.

I stood on the patio, put my finger on the ignition, and said, "Gentleman, start your grill." Not even a spark. So I called, paradoxically, the hot line and spoke with a very nice customer service representative named Savanna.

"I'm not a griller," admitted Savanna, who had been on the job for only four months. "I've never tried. I didn't know that gas tanks expired until I started working here. I've learned so much."

One of the things she learned was the bubble test.

"Get a spray bottle with soap and water and spray the hose and regulator to see if there's a gas leak," Savanna said.

"I've never even taken a bubble bath," I said while doing as instructed. No bubbles, bubbles, but there was toil and trouble, which entailed lighting a match and trying, futilely, to start the grill that way.

"Apparently, there's not a leak, but we'll send you a free replacement hose and regulator anyway," said Savanna, who got the apparatus to me in about week.

When it arrived, I fetched a wrench and, while removing the original hose and regulator, gashed my middle finger. It was appropriate.

After stanching a Niagara-like torrent of blood, I got the new thingamajig attached. Then I tried to start the grill.

It was still the mechanical equivalent of a mime. I wanted to hit it with the wrench but feared it would erupt like the Hindenburg, causing Sue to exclaim, "Oh, the stupidity!"

The next day, I called the hot line again and this time spoke with an equally nice representative named Nipa, who is a vegetarian and, like Savanna, doesn't grill.

I gave her the whole sad story. Nipa listened patiently and said, "Remove the ignition button." I did. Then she said, "Is there a battery in there?"

"No," I answered sheepishly.

"Get a double-A battery and put it in," Nipa instructed. "Insert the negative first and the positive facing the cap."

Voila! The grill started on the first try.

"You're a genius," I told Nipa, who was too polite to say that I'm not. "And you're invited over for our first cookout on the new grill. I'll even make you some veggies."

"Thank you," Nipa said. "What can I bring?"

"How about some batteries?" I suggested. "Without them, I wouldn't be cooking with gas."

"Strawberry Fields for Joking"

If I were to write a nursery rhyme about a garrulous geezer on a fruitful foray with his giddy granddaughters, it would go like this: "Punny Poppie picked a peck of perfect produce."

That precious pair of pumpkins, Chloe and Lilly, are the apples of my eye. Actually, both eyes, since there are two of them. And we love to go pumpkin and apple picking, though not at the same time because I couldn't lug that much fruit without collapsing in a field of screams.

But we found ourselves in strawberry fields — not forever, but for an hour's worth of picking pleasure.

Chloe, Lilly, and I were accompanied by Sue and Lauren. We all wore masks, except to take pictures, and kept a social distance from other strawberry pickers, primarily to ensure physical safety but also to protect the mental health of innocent bystanders who might otherwise be exposed to my stupid jokes.

Like this one:

Me: "Knock, knock."

Chloe and Lilly: "Who's there?"

Me: "Berry."

Chloe and Lilly: "Berry who?"

Me: "We're having a berry good time!"

Chloe and Lilly giggled. Other pickers picked up the pace.

Two who bravely didn't were a very nice woman named Jenny and her equally nice granddaughter, Abby.

"Hi!" Chloe chirped. "My name is Chloe and this is my sister, Lilly. What's your name?"

"Jenny," said Jenny.

"What's your name?" Chloe asked Abby.

"Abby," said Abby.

"Nice to meet you," said Chloe, who pointed to me and said, "This is my grandfather, Poppie."

"Hi, Poppie," said Jenny.

"Hi, Grammy," I replied when she told me what Abby calls her. "Are you a singer?"

"I wish," said Jenny.

"I can sing," said Abby.

"You must be good," I said. "You have a Grammy."

That joke and another one I told about not being Chuck Berry went over Abby's head (she's short), but that didn't stop Chloe from repeating my earlier one: "We're having a berry good time!"

Jenny and Abby laughed.

"Chloe is funny," Jenny said. "She must take after her grandfather."

Sue and Lauren shook their heads and kept walking.

After saying goodbye to Jenny and Abby, the girls and I took a strawberry shortcut, moving over to an untouched row to select the plumpest, juiciest berries.

"Look at mine, Poppie!" exclaimed Lilly, who tossed away a few that weren't up to her standards and filled her basket with only perfect pickings.

Chloe also had discerning tastes and even faster fingers, loading her basket in what must have been record time.

After an hour, the Strawberry Alarm Clock went off in my head and we headed back to our cars. On the way, Chloe introduced herself to a girl named April, who said she has a brother named Colton. As he passed by, Chloe said, "Your name is Colton!"

The kid blanched and said, "How did you know?"

"You're famous," I told him.

He stared at me incredulously.

"Your sister told me," Chloe explained. "Look at our strawberries!"

"Wow," said Colton.

"We left some for you out in the field," I said. "But you better hurry up. They're going fast."

Colton looked at me warily and walked away.

We stopped at the stand for an orchard pie filled with blueberries, raspberries, and, of course, strawberries.

When we got to our cars, Lauren said she was going to use her berries to make smoothies for the girls.

Sue said she was going to make strawberry shortcake.

After popping a sweet berry into my mouth, I said I was going to make my own creation: strawberry daiquiris.

"After listening to your stupid jokes," Sue said, "I could use one."

CHAPTER 10

"Retirement Is Going to Work"

(How can you be retired if you're not actually retired? Ask Sue, who planned to retire but got sidetracked, first by my buyout and then by the quarantine, which was like being — you guessed it — retired.)

I used to think that the greatest gig in America was the concept of "suspended with pay." It's when someone (I always hoped it would be me) did something bad enough at work that he or she would be told not to come into the office anymore but would still be on the payroll.

What would I have to do to get that — pretend to be Moe of the Three Stooges and poke my boss in the eyes?

Now that I'm retired, I don't have to wonder about it anymore. But I've come to believe that another great gig is the concept of "working remotely."

That's what Sue started doing when the pandemic struck. Her birthday is November 10, the same as my mother's, except my mother is older. Sue wanted to reach sixty-six, when she could get the Social Security max, and work through the end of the school year in June.

Then, with a nod to Alice Cooper, school not only would be out for summer, it would be out forever.

But it was still in because the virus crisis closed the building, meaning Sue wouldn't have to go to work but would still have to do some work.

That involved attending online seminars, participating in Zoom meetings, and coordinating with the classroom teacher on lessons, including videos in which Sue told the kids about such educational activities as growing flowers, doing arts and crafts, and caring for a pet, which in our case isn't a dog or a cat but a fish that actually swam up to the side of the bowl and smiled for the camera.

It was the best of both worlds: Sue would still be on the payroll, but she wouldn't have to get up at 5:30 every weekday morning.

"It's like being retired," she said. "I can sleep in, do just a little work, and get paid. When school reopens, I'll quit."

The downside: She was stuck in the house with me.

"I always thought I'd retire first," Sue said.

"You're older than I am," I pointed out.

"By two months and a day," she said.

"Yes, but we were born in different years," I countered.

My birthday, January 11, is shared with only one famous person, Alexander Hamilton, which means I will either have a hit Broadway show or be killed in a duel.

"You're definitely not a banker," Sue said.

When I retired, I was busier than when I was working. I went down to D.C. five times in four and a half months (twice with Sue, three times solo) to help Katie and Dave with Xavier, Zoe, and Quinn. I also helped Lauren and Guillaume with Chloe and Lilly.

I was The Manny, a big-baby babysitter, living in a grandfather's paradise.

Then came the holidays, then the pandemic struck, then I started doubling up on my columns, then I began writing this book, all while working on a sitcom that I have been shopping around, hoping to find an agent or a producer who is either foolish or drunk enough to go for it.

Because she was still going to work, Sue missed out on watching the kids. When we were quarantined, neither of us could babysit, see our daughters, or do much of anything except spend every day with each other.

"Is this what retirement is going to be like?" Sue wondered on more than one occasion.

The upside for her is that on most mornings, I get up first to make the coffee.

"It's better than mine," Sue acknowledged.

"This is probably the only thing I do better than you," I said, sipping a cup of steaming, delicious java.

Sue nodded, smiled, and took a sip from her cup.

As the days passed and we settled into a routine, which included sharing the computer for our various projects, boredom began to creep in.

"I love you," Sue has told me, "but it's tough spending every day with you. You're the only person I see."

That was the nub of the problem: Retirement was a great prospect, as long as there was the freedom to do things, both together and separately. It's tough to pull off when you're quarantined.

"I need to find something," Sue said. "A little job, maybe."

She had planned to substitute-teach after she called it quits, but now she won't go back.

"I don't want to have to battle the traffic again," Sue said. "And I'd get calls early in the morning, almost every weekday, to come in. Plus, with the virus still out there, I don't want to take a chance."

Since she couldn't see the grandkids and she couldn't get out to do things, she needed a purpose.

After all these years, I'm still what I have always wanted to be: a newspaper humorist. I'm grateful that even in retirement, I have my dream job.

Sue has always loved children, but she doesn't want to teach anymore. She's smart, with the talent to do anything she wants. I told her that she'd find something.

What we both have found is that, for all the annoyances, we greatly enjoy being together. Our love has not faded. In fact, it's stronger because Sue has learned to put up with my stupid jokes, which I told at work before I retired but which I now tell incessantly around the house.

As for Sue's annoying tendencies — well, aside from leaving the cap off the toothpaste, which really irritates me, there aren't any.

By the time you read this, Sue will probably be retired. What's definite is that we don't go to work anymore. For years, that's what we dreamed about. Now our dreams have come true.

So tomorrow morning, like every morning, we'll sleep later than we used to and ease into the day.

And, best of all for Sue, I'll get up first to make the coffee.

EPILOGUE

Before I retired, TGIF stood for Thank God It's Friday. Now it stands for Thank God I'm Free.

Still, days can put you in a daze. When you're not working anymore, it's easy to forget what day it is.

That's not true when you're on the job. In fact, it's impossible to lose track of days.

Take Monday — please. For the working man or woman, it's the worst day because it is, of course, the beginning of the workweek.

I chose to take a positive view. As I always told my colleagues, "Monday is my seventh-favorite day of the week."

Some smiled. Some shrugged. Some looked like they were about to throw up.

Tuesday wasn't great, but at least it was better than Monday. One down, four to go.

Though an improvement over Monday and Tuesday, Wednesday was bad because it was known as "hump day." If you said that to the wrong person, you could find yourself in the human resources department.

I usually breezed through Monday and Tuesday (when you work hard to avoid work, it's easy), but Wednesday put me in the homestretch for doing the work that needed to be done by the end of the week.

Thursday was also busy, but at least there was a light at the end of the tunnel. I just hoped it wasn't from an oncoming train.

Then, praise the Lord, Friday arrived.

"TGIF!" everyone would say.

But it wasn't always wonderful because it dragged on more than any other day of the workweek.

I'll briefly skip over to Sunday, which was a day off but wasn't enjoyable by mid-afternoon because I started thinking about Monday.

Sue dreaded it even more than I did.

"Ugh!" she'd moan. "I have to get up at 5:30 tomorrow morning."

And it started all over again: rising but not shining, chugging a cup of coffee, wolfing down breakfast, taking a shower, getting dressed, and heading out to battle rush-hour traffic so you could plant yourself at a desk where a week's worth of work awaited.

That brings me to Saturday, by far the best day of the week.

It's when you could sleep late, enjoy a big breakfast, ease into the day, do some chores around the house, have leftovers for lunch, maybe go shopping, do some yard work, or sack out in a hammock, and end up going out for a burger or ordering a pizza for dinner. At night, there'd be a movie, usually seen at home because real life is seldom lived in the fast lane.

But after you stop working, all the days blur into each other. You might sleep in on Tuesday or do Saturday chores on Thursday. And Monday doesn't seem so bad anymore.

As Sue said one weekday afternoon while we relaxed in our favorite chairs, "I always looked forward to the weekend. Now we have it all the time."

"When you're retired," I said, with a wide smile and a glass of wine, "every day is Saturday."

Printed in the United States
By Bookmasters